How to Get HIM

to Put That Ring on Your Finger in 365 Days or Less

Glenda A. Wallace

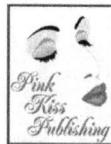

Pink Kiss Publishing

Pink Kiss Publishing Company
Gautier, Mississippi

Interior designed by: Glenda Wallace at interiorbookdesigns.com
Cover by: Donna Osborn Clark at CreationbyDonna.com

ISBN: 978-0-9835756-0-3
Library of Congress Control Number: 2014907360

Published by:
Pink Kiss Publishing Company
P.O. Box 744
Gautier, Mississippi 39553
(228) 366-6829
www.pinkkisspublishing.com

To everyone who believes in love…

Acknowledgments

I would like to thank the many individuals who contributed to the writing of this book, both directly and indirectly. Many of you have shared so much of yourselves with me over the years, and many of us have developed a wonderful friendship. For that, I am truly grateful.

To my family, thank you for your undying love and continued support in everything that I do. I love you guys!

To that special man in my life, I thank God for bringing us together. Through our love, I learn something new every day. You are truly one of a kind, and I'm so thankful that you're mine. I love you with all my heart.

Most importantly, to my Lord and Savior Jesus Christ; I thank You, and I love You because without You, *none* of this would be possible. I owe You my life!

Contents

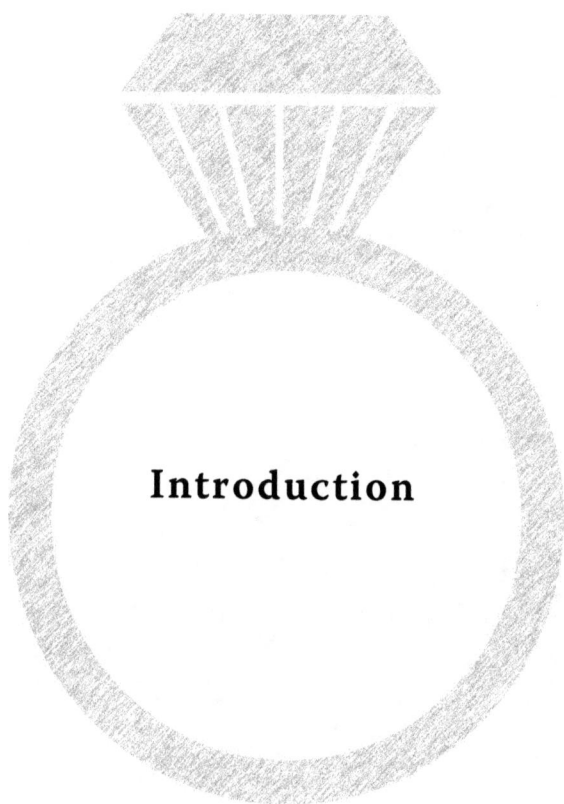

Introduction

hat makes men marry? Single women all over the world have been perplexed by this question for ages. I came up with the concept of this book after many years of learning what works when getting a man to commit to marriage. I'm often asked, "What makes your book different than other 'How-to' books?" Well, I will be the first to admit that I can't teach you to do something that I've never done. For example, I will never write a book about the joys of childbirth, because I've never had a child. I wouldn't write a book about how to earn a million dollars when I've yet to earn my first million. Furthermore, *you* wouldn't go out and buy a book that teaches how to earn a million written by an author who hasn't, simply because it would be hard to accept their credibility. However, it's no secret that I've been married five times, and proposed to a total of eighteen times. Over the years, I have perfected a foolproof technique that is guaranteed to gain results for anyone. Even you!

I decided to write this book after publishing my first book, *I Need Therapy* in 2007. I wrote this book as a companion book because many women had additional questions and topics that they wanted to address.

I Need Therapy addresses the *root* of relationship problems. It teaches the principles of how to develop and achieve self-confidence, so that we can build healthier relationships by beginning with "self." It is filled with an insurmountable amount of valuable information on how a woman should begin the task of the getting the man she wants to marry her by first working on herself. After all, it begins with you.

You must make yourself an asset to a man in order for him to want you as a wife, and there are many facets to consider when you aim to become the "total" package. I am going to make it real simple for any woman to get that special man to put that ring on her finger in 365 days or less, because in this book, I'm going to break down each of those facets in detail.

Some women feel that a man should marry her just because they are in a relationship. Unfortunately, men don't think that way. Selecting a wife is a much more involved process for a man than just being in a relationship.

I Need Therapy was written to serve many purposes. Originally, it was designed to be a woman's empowerment guide. The primary purpose was to encourage women to make better decisions in their everyday lives. Not just with their relationships, but also with their health and financial matters. It addresses sensitive subjects such as infidelity, how to survive when the relationship or marriage is over, revenge, drama, dating a married man, how to protect our children from the predators that *we* bring into our homes, men who are living on the down low, as well as how to develop and achieve self-confidence and build self-esteem. This book is a continuation of that process. You will also find that many lessons are carried over from *I Need Therapy* for the benefit of those who haven't read it and as a refresher course for those who have.

Since publishing my first book, I have received hundreds of emails and letters from women asking for advice on how to convince their man to commit to marriage. There were also a significant number of single women who contacted me with their dating dilemmas about finding Mr. Right. This book was created with those women in mind. It addresses a vast range of issues that they expressed to me.

This book is filled with stories and examples based off the questions you wanted answers to. Let's face it, this type of book is so popular because relationship problems will always exist. The most important thing is to understand how to handle problems when they arise.

Most of the women who contacted me are suffering from what I call *normal* relationship problems. However, we all know that when a problem exists in *your* relationship, there is nothing normal about it. When I refer to normal relationship problems, I mean the common complaints about a man; he's not romantic, he won't talk to me, he won't listen to my needs, etc. These are common complaints that women have about the men in their lives. But it doesn't have to be the deciding factor in ending a relationship or marriage.

Believe it or not, I also received many comments and emails from men thanking me for writing *I Need Therapy*. Some men confessed to purchasing the book as a gag gift for their wives, girlfriends, sisters and co-workers as if to say, "Yeah, you do need therapy." However, after noticing changes the women in their lives exhibited after reading the book, many men wanted to know what was printed on those pages that could inspire changes in behavior that some of them have been living with for years.

Some claimed they found the book to be right on point, and admitted that I do have a lot of insight into what men are looking for from their relationships and marriage. Many thanked me for writing a book that was helpful in getting their women to better understand how they think about certain issues relating to their relationships.

Personally, I'm pleased that so many men found *I Need Therapy* to be helpful in improving the quality of their relationships. Finally, many guys stated that reading the book also helped them to better understand how women think. For me, that in itself was an accomplishment. As with *I Need Therapy*, I hope men find some of the principles outlined in this book helpful in understanding women and why we act as we do.

Although this book was written as a guide for women who are looking to get married, the same principles also apply to women already married and just need some helpful pointers on keeping their marriage fresh and alive. Sometimes when we have been with a man for a while, we have a tendency to forget the old saying "What you do to get him, you must also do to keep him". This book will serve as a reminder of how important it is to continue to nurture your relationship even *after* you get that ring.

Anyone who has ever been in a relationship knows that problems occur. Make no mistake about it. Additionally, just as many men suffer with relationship problems as women do. The only difference is that men deal with problems in their own way because they are wired differently than women. Relationship problems exist because of those vast differences between men and women. We don't think alike, act alike or respond to situations in the same way. We have different perceptions of *how* problems should be handled. Even our expectations are different. However, we can learn to have better, healthier relationships when we learn to respect and accept each other's differences.

This book is about change. It is going to open your mind to change how you think, thereby, changing how you act. If what you're doing is not working, it is time to try something different. If you have purchased this book, you are taking the first step to making some valuable changes in your life.

In this book, I will address the many ways in which we can begin to bridge the communicate gap between men and women, so that we can achieve a common goal of having healthier, happier relationships.

I'm no different than many of you. I've gone through my share of failed relationships. I've suffered from low self-esteem and lack of self-confidence as a result of some of those relationships. In my younger days, I didn't care if my relationships worked. If the man I was with didn't get it together, it was easy for me to walk away. I knew I could always get another man *better* than the last.

We are all human and we all have our share of faults, but when I was so unhappy with one man's faults I would move on to the next man, determined to get it right in the next *new* relationship, determined to find that one *good* man. Unfortunately, the next man came with his own set of issues.

Eventually, I noticed a pattern starting to develop in me. I was becoming the type of woman who would walk away from any relationship that wasn't working on every level. Each situation was the same. I would complain until I was blue in the face about what *I* needed from *him*. I would be ready to do battle with him when he didn't know how to communicate in a manner that I understood. Finally, after feeling that I had invested too much time and energy on something that couldn't be fixed, I would walk away; hence, the five marriages and subsequent divorces.

So, I continued my quest to find that one good man, and for the life of me, I couldn't figure it out! Why were all of these men defective? It took me a while to discover that everyone is defective in their own way, me included. Looking back, I realize all of my exes are wonderful men. There was something unique about each one that I loved dearly, but they also possessed their own set of flaws, that at some point, I no longer cared to deal with. Unfortunately, when I felt frustrated with the knowledge that I couldn't do anything to correct their flaws, I would once again walk away.

It took some time for me to learn that everyone has faults, and to recognize that I do, too. But part of the growth process is being able to accept responsibility for the role that you played in a relationship that is no longer working. As I look back on my own experiences, I realize that I played a huge role in the demise of those relationships.

One of my biggest flaws was my lack of patience, which made it easy for me to walk away. Over the past few years, I have taken the time to examine what marriage and relationships really means to me. I learned to take my own advice. I had to take a step back, look at my life and say, "Okay, what am I doing wrong here?" It took some time, but God gave me my answers. I had to be honest with myself and take responsibility for the choices I had made in my life. I had to learn patience. I learned to look beyond what I "expected" and "wanted" in a man and a relationship, and opened my eyes to see him for who he really is. And I had to stop making excuses for the behavior of others. I wasted so many years trying to fix the men in my life when all I ever had to do was fix *me*. The biggest lesson I learned? I learned that *all relationships are not meant to result in marriage.* Some relationships are meant to teach you about who you really are.

As I look back, I realize that in every situation that led to the demise of my previous marriages, I could have controlled the outcome by following a few simple steps. Had I taken those steps, I could have saved myself a lot of heartache, because in many cases, I already knew his faults *before* I committed myself to a long-term relationship or marriage.

Today, I follow those steps by taking responsibility for myself and my future. After being married five times you become extremely cautious. It is easy to feel like there is no room for error, and although I do expect to marry again, all of the steps have to be in place from the onset or I refuse to do it. Today, I own up to the mistakes of my past. Today, I am a better woman *because* of my past, not in spite of it. Being in love "now" I am happier than I have ever been in my life, mainly because the lessons of my past made me the woman that I am today. I can appreciate everything about the man in my life and the intimacy between us is unlike anything I have ever experienced before in my life.

As you read this book, not only are you getting the benefit of learning what always came to me so effortlessly, you are also getting the benefit of the lessons that I've learned about how to create a successful relationship. And it all starts with "YOU!"

I don't have a background in psychotherapy or psychology, and I am not an expert on relationships or human behavior, but I feel that after five marriages and eighteen marriage proposals I am qualified to share what I've learned from my experiences with all of you.

Some people feel that psychologist, therapist and counselor have all the answers. It is true that these people are trained and qualified in human behavior, but that alone doesn't mean that they have all the answers. If so, they wouldn't face many of the same relationship problems that we face.

For example, I was contacted by a twenty-nine year old woman from Miami, Florida who was concerned because she had never been in a serious long-term relationship. She was afraid that she would never marry, even though she dated frequently, was very successful, and had no children. She said when men ask her out, after the first date they never call her again and she didn't understand why. She suspected that these men were all intimidated by her success. That's when I learned she was a family and marriage counselor. Imagine that! Someone having a career as a family and marriage counselor who has never actually been married!

It proves a point, you can have all the training in the world, but if you haven't lived it, or if you haven't had the hands-on life experience, it's hard to give someone advice about it.

When I developed breast cancer, my doctors gave me all of this great advice about what I should expect as a result of the chemotherapy; the uncontrollable nausea, hair loss and possible weight loss because I wouldn't have an appetite. Yet, when I started my treatments, I found that some of the things they told me to expect never happened. But because they were the experts and knew what they were talking about, I accepted the fate of my disease without question.

I was scheduled to begin my first round of chemotherapy three days before Thanksgiving 2001. I found myself dreading that particular Thanksgiving because I knew I wouldn't be able to enjoy the traditional Thanksgiving dinner with my family. I was forewarned by my doctors that I would spend the next few weeks extremely nauseous.

After that first round of chemotherapy, I found myself sitting at home watching the clock thinking to myself... *according to my doctors, I should be getting sick right about now.* Needless to say, it never happened, but I found myself waiting to get sick based on what the "experts" told me. As it turns out, I never got sick and I had a wonderful Thanksgiving with my family. In fact, instead of losing weight as I went through my cancer treatments, I gained twenty pounds. Although my doctors were trained in their field, they had never had breast cancer, so they couldn't tell me precisely what I would go through, or how my body would react to the chemotherapy and my disease. They couldn't predict how I would feel as a result of my treatments.

My point is, in any situation you have to keep an open mind and be cautious of who you take, not just relationship advice from, but be cautious of who you take *any* advice from. In addition, when you take advice, don't look at it as law. Every person's experiences are as unique and different as we are.

It was never my intention to become a relationship author. However, after releasing *I Need Therapy*, I received many emails and letters from women who had either read the book or read an article or short story about relationships on one of my websites or blogs. In addition, I also host a weekly Internet radio talk show *"The G- Spot!"* on Blog Talk Radio where my co-host, Ms. LaTonya Armstrong, and I discuss many relationship topics that come directly from our dedicated readers and listeners.

I found that when women have issues they want to talk about it. On the show we have an open forum and we discuss many topics women find important. Sometimes women want my opinion and sometimes they only want to vent about an issue to an impartial person. After all, in many cases, it is harder to discuss personal issues with close friends or family members. So, this is how I *accidentally* fell into talking about relationships. Keep in mind that it is okay to use any outlet that works for you. If calling my radio show and talking about a particular problem or issue helps you, then by all means do. If you need the support of your girlfriends, do that. Women need support when dealing with our problems and frustrations that we may not get at home from our men. So by all means, continue to use these channels as a way of releasing those pent up emotions.

What I find even more amazing is that men also call in with their relationship problems. They show up in the chat room and call into my show to talk about their issues. Many times, they want women to know how they think and feel about those issues.

Everything I do is about bridging the gap between the sexes, so that we can have a better understanding of each other. Furthermore, I do it in a way that is easy for everyone to understand. By keeping it real! It is so rewarding when I receive letters from each gender who say that my book or advice literally saved their relationship, marriage, and in some cases, even their life.

When I originally wrote *I Need Therapy*, I wrote it to help women who were experiencing similar issues dealing with men, love, and relationships. I believe that women share a common bond. In many ways we are all the same woman. Although we may be separated by age, race, religion, and culture—along with social and economic status—women share many common traits. We experience many of the same problems with men, love, and relationships. In *I Need Therapy* my purpose was to explore those common bonds of sisterhood to say to women: "No matter what you may be going through, you are not alone." When you are experiencing an issue, don't feel that you are the only one.

Shortly before my first book was released, a beautiful, vibrant thirty-something-year-old woman decided to take her own life by jumping to her death from the sixth floor parking garage at the casino where I worked. It was a devastating blow to everyone around because the people closest to her never knew she had issues so severe she would actually consider taking her own life.

Every day I wonder if there was one word that someone could have said that might have prevented her from making that fatal decision. We never know what demons others wrestle with in their minds, and my writing has always been my way of reaching out to women who may need to hear an encouraging word—by letting her know that she has a world full of sisters who experience some of the same issues. All women need to know that there *is* a better way of handling our issues in life – stress, depression, anger, etc. Most of the time, these are issues that are difficult to deal with alone, and the male species are not equipped to handle these issues. It is wonderful if you have a man in your life who will support you through your issues, but if not, reach out to someone that you can trust; a girlfriend, family member or member of your church. And if you feel you might harm yourself or someone else, please reach out to a physician to address your feelings.

Again, although I am not an expert in the field of psychotherapy or psychology, I do consider myself an expert in life experiences. I speak of my experiences when I talk about relationships. I speak about the things that I've gone through, and the lessons that I have learned. I speak of the studies I have conducted and the one-on-one interviews I have done with men and women. My friends jokingly refer to me as a modern-day relationship philosopher, but who really cares about the title as long as the principles work. When I initially started interviewing men back in the 1980s to gather data for my first book, my original mission was to find out what captured a man's attention when it came to women. I wanted to know what their wants, needs and desires were within a relationship. I found that men are more than happy to tell you what he looks for in a woman, if you only ask.

My purpose in wanting this information was twofold; I wanted to know because I was writing a book, and because I wanted to be the best woman I could be for my potential man. At the time, I was nineteen and had never been in an intimate relationship with a man. (Yeah, I was an old virgin) All of the information that I gathered was extremely helpful to me. I interviewed many different men; black, white, Hispanic, Asian, young and old. It didn't matter, I was on a mission. I wanted answers and I was taking notes. I have done my research, and all of the information that I gained over the years is compiled within this book.

This book came about as a result of women contacting me and saying, "Hey, I'm ready to get married, but I can't get one man to commit to marriage. How the hell do *you* do it?" I get very different reactions from men *and* women when I tell them I have been married five times and proposed to a total of eighteen times. Most men are intrigued; they want to know what it is about me that made five men want to make me their wife. Most women are curious; they want to know what I did and how I did it, in order to get five men to make a commitment to marriage. I often hear from women who say, "I can't get *one* man to marry me and you've had five! Is there something wrong with me? Is there something I'm not doing right?"

Just because you're not married, and have never been proposed to, doesn't mean there is something wrong with you. You may not be aware of what men are looking for when selecting a wife. Half the time most men don't know what they are looking for in a wife until it's staring them in the face. This fact was confirmed on my radio show recently where we asked men about that subject. Our topic was "What Men Want and Need from Their Women and Relationships!" Most men agreed that it can be difficult for a man to tell a woman what his needs are when he may not know. Yet, they all agreed that once he finds it, he will know.

However, most people agree that five marriages and eighteen marriage proposals is not normal by any standard. Usually, the initial reaction I get from people (especially women) is, *"What's your secret?"* The truth is there is no secret. It is important for women to recognize that there is not just one thing that a woman must do, but a combination of things that gain results. A woman's only objective is to master that combination in order to mold herself into that well-rounded woman that any man couldn't possibly resist.

In addition, before you start thinking that this book is all about sex, it's not! A smart woman knows that sex alone will not make a man want to marry her. I don't care how good it is. Sex alone will not *keep* a man. If it did, there wouldn't be so many "baby mamas" out there; they would be wives. But, I will address what role sex actually plays in getting your man to put that ring on your finger in a later chapter.

This book is designed to teach you about who *you* really are. It will teach you everything you need to know in order to get your man to put that ring on your finger. My writing is raw, direct, and straight to the point, and in this book, you will find a lot of real talk. You will find that I'm not like most authors who use fancy words to try to pretty-up the scenarios. As I have experienced it, I will tell it. As it comes to me, I will relay it to you. I keep it simple because it is my sincere desire to simplify my writing so everyone can understand what is written on the pages of this book. No matter your age, race, social or economic status, I want every woman to understand the messages outlined in this book. I want every *single* woman to be able to achieve her dreams of marrying the man she desires.

I will address every aspect of relationships, from the initial meeting, to how men and women relate to each other on a social level, sex, and finally – if it comes down to it – knowing when it's time to throw in the towel and admit defeat. Yeah, I know some of you might not want to hear that, but as you go through this book remember my most important lesson. *All relationships are not meant to result in marriage.*

Using my tips might get your man to marry you, but it doesn't mean that he is the one for you. So don't pick and choose ideas throughout the book; read it in its entirety. If you do, you will find that it will help you learn more about yourself. It will help you to recognize when a situation is not healthy for you.

I know that some of us are stubborn and we want to do what we want to do. Ladies, just remember that this was my problem when I was younger. So read the book, really absorb the material, examine the lessons, and apply the principles. In doing so, you might find that you actually like who *you* really are.

I will also address how some women feel that most men are dogs and players. The fact is, ladies, in this game of life everyone possesses the ability to be a player, even you. So we are going to learn to change the way we think, thereby, changing our negative opinions about men in general. We will learn to change our method of selection, thereby, eliminating those who seek to play games with us. By the end of this book you will clearly be able to identify the signs that men exhibit when they choose to play games. Remember, there is good and bad in everyone and men are not dogs!

For most women, trying to understand men can be tiresome, frustrating and can sometimes make you wonder if going through all the effort is really worth it.

Ladies, men are really not as complicated as you think, but in order to understand how he thinks you must get on his level. You must put yourself in his place and think like he thinks. Studies have shown that women are smarter than men, so it might take some effort on your part to think like he does. However, when you learn to understand the way men think, you can and will drastically improve the quality of your relationship.

Ever wonder why some women marry while others never do? Or have you wondered how self-proclaimed bachelors suddenly find themselves at the altar? Well, I've done studies and tested theories that will help you to understand how men actually think about relationships, sex and marriage.

The one thing most women seem to agree on is that in most cases, getting a man to commit is no easy feat. I don't care what his situation may be; most men seem to run from the commitment of marriage. He may or may not be attractive, he may or may not have a nickel in his pocket, yet, he will run. But do not get discouraged. It is not impossible to persuade a man to commit.

In fact, I'll tell you a secret, I have never met a man who wouldn't commit and I've dated men from all spectrums; professional athletes, celebrities, as well as the average, every day Joe!

The truth is most men are not commitment phobic. Fact is, a man will commit when he finds what he is looking for. He may be with you, but may not want a lifelong commitment with you. Whereas, he may breakup with you and marry the next women he gets involved with.

For example, my friend Jessica was engaged to a man for six years. He broke up with her to be with another woman. He married the new woman within six months of meeting her. Needless to say, my girlfriend was crushed. Obviously, she wasn't what he was looking for in a wife. The qualities he was looking for he found somewhere else. This is one of many examples of a man committing to a woman when he finds what he's looking for.

My principles contained in this book will work for anyone. I don't care what you look like, how old you are, what you do for a living, how much money you make or how many children you may have; my system *will* work for you!

I didn't get five husbands and eighteen marriage proposals because I'm cute. In fact, when it comes to looks, I'm quite ordinary. But I did it by taking the time to educate myself on what men really want in their relationships. The men that I've been in relationships with usually start discussing marriage within the first six months, without me ever bringing up the subject, dropping hints, or leaving wedding planner guides on the coffee table.

I will also address the different stages of relationships and what to expect at each stage. You will learn that a man will be able to judge if you are wife material within a certain amount of time, and you will also be able to gauge, without guessing, if he views you as wife material.

Make no mistake about it; attaining your goal will require some work. Fortunately, I've already done the hard part, now it is up to you to implement the rules. But, there *is* some work involved.

Remember, the key to obtaining the things you want in life begins with *YOU*; whether it's a house, car, job, or even a husband. No matter what your situation may be, you have the ability to achieve your dreams. So, if you're prepared and willing to make the necessary changes needed to obtain that goal, let's get started on a journey that will change your life!

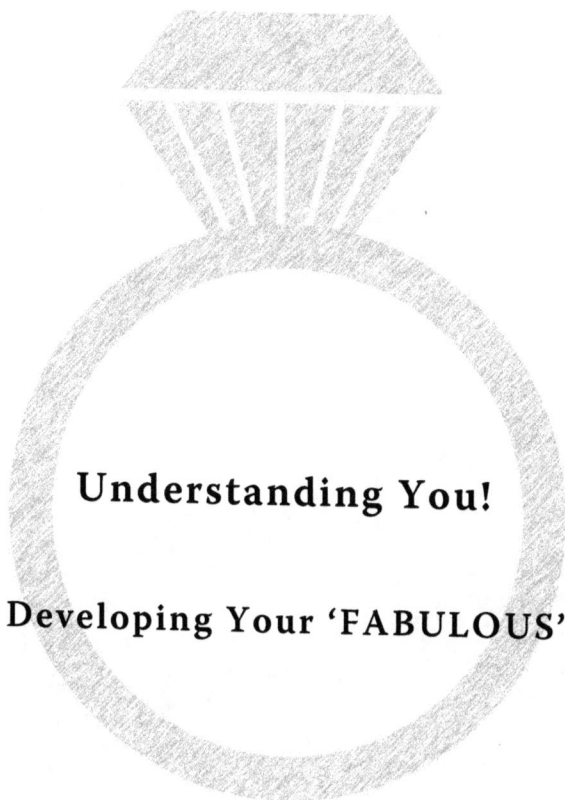

Understanding You!

(And Developing Your 'FABULOUS' Self)

So here we are, the fact that you are reading this book means that you are either dating and want to know what you can do to elevate your relationship status with your man to the point of making a commitment to marriage, or you are single and want to know how to go about finding and capturing the attention of that special man whom you desire a long-term commitment or marriage with. Maybe it's neither of those. Maybe you are already married and just want some pointers on how to strengthen the marriage you are already in. Whatever your reasons are for reading this book, we're going to start from the root of where all relationship problems begin, with YOU!

I'm sure that most of you will agree that relationships are not easy. Sometimes it seems that everyone you meet comes with some sort of emotional baggage. Whether it is child support issues, baby mama or baby daddy drama, police records/convictions, bankruptcies, bad credit, you name it, somebody is going through it.

We all come with baggage because nobody is squeaky clean. We all have a past and because of our past, we are bound to have some issues that carry over into our relationships. When we go into a new relationship most of us carry that baggage with us.

Ladies, please believe me when I say you are not the only one dealing with drama or baggage in your life. This is not an age thing. I have received letters from twenty-year-olds and fifty-year-olds alike who are going through it. It is not a race thing. I receive emails from Caucasian, Asian, Hispanic and African-American women. All of whom have had some kind of issue, which resulted in some sort of drama all because of someone's baggage.

As a single woman, I didn't want to be a burden to the next man I became involved with. Therefore, it was up to me to take the necessary steps to assure that I wasn't. The question remains, how did I do it? I did it by getting myself together. This is why we're going to start this process by focusing on ourselves.

When it comes to establishing a relationship, the first thing a woman should consider is if she is mentally and emotionally ready for a commitment. It is important to evaluate your reasons for wanting to get into a relationship, because sometimes, without being aware, it is easy to allow circumstances to nudge you into a situation that you may not be ready for.

For example, you have been dating a new man for a couple of weeks; he gets kicked out of his apartment and now needs somewhere to live. Since you are already dating you offer to let him stay at your place. Next thing you know, you are in a full-blown relationship and never had time to establish that he was the one you wanted to be with.

Many times you can find yourself locked into a relationship when all you initially wanted to do was date. However, you went out, had sex on the first night and a few weeks later you find out that you're pregnant. Now suddenly, you are in a relationship. This is especially true of younger ladies. Young ladies, it is okay to take your time and date different men. Dating provides you an opportunity to learn what you like and want in a man. Personally, I don't think anyone should marry during their early to mid-twenties, even if you actively dated as a teenager. You will find that what you liked as a teenager is vastly different from what you'll like as a woman.

I'll use myself as an example. I had my first sexual relationship at the age of nineteen. I joined the military at twenty and was married for the first time at age twenty-one. So tell me, with my limited experience with men, what did I know about marriage? Furthermore, what did I really know about men? How was it possible for me to make a proper selection of a mate or husband when I had no idea what I wanted or needed from a relationship or marriage?

This is why it is so important to set some parameters and establish what your expectations are before you allow yourself to become overly involved. Ask yourself the following questions: Why do I want a relationship? Am I mentally and emotionally ready to be in a relationship? (This includes making sure your baggage has been properly stored away and/or disposed of). What are my expectations for my relationship?

You should be able to come up with a concrete answer to those questions. If you are unable to, or if you're doing it for any of the following reasons, then you are not ready.

✓ **You are doing it for financial security.**

This happens quite frequently. A woman might get into a relationship because she is looking for someone to take care of her financially. Also, many women stay in relationships that are not working for the same reason. They become dependent, and although the relationship may be unhealthy, she may find it difficult to let go. Understand that before you can begin to find true happiness you have to let go of something that is not working on all levels.

✓ **To get out of a relationship or get over your last relationship.**

I find that this is more common with men, as they find it hard to let go of a current relationship until they find a replacement. However, it also happens with women. It brings to mind the saying: "Never quit a job until you find another one."

Many people have a fear of being alone, so when a relationship ends there is a desperate need to find a replacement as quickly as possible. But when one relationship ends you need time to heal before you begin another relationship. This also has a lot to do with that emotional baggage that we talked about earlier. People don't believe in taking the necessary time between relationships to figure it all out. You break-up one day and the following day you've already changed your Internet profile status to reflect that you are: looking for friends, dating, and serious relationships. Are you kidding me?

For some people, not being in a relationship makes them feel like a failure, as if they are not worthy enough of being loved. You must realize that not being in a relationship does not make you a failure. Yeah, I know there are many women out there in relationships and marriages who have a habit of looking down their noses at single women who are not in a relationship. But don't get caught up worrying about what others think about you. We expend too much energy worrying about how people see us, and life is too short to get caught up in that. For those women who feel superior just because you are married or in a committed relationship, please remember that life carries no guarantees. There are many women who were in your shoes and happened to suddenly discover that her man was leaving to be with someone else. So never put your relationship status on a pedestal and think you are above the next woman just because you already have the ring. Put yourself in another woman's shoes. How would you react if you woke up and found yourself suddenly single again?

✔ **To make you feel better about yourself.**

Many women experience the effects of low self-esteem at some point in their lives. Women are emotional creatures by nature and our emotional balance is easily upset. Most anything can make us feel inadequate, not quite good enough and unworthy. A woman who suffers from low self-esteem may feel inadequate about what she has to bring or offer to a relationship. She may use a relationship to make her feel better about herself. She might define her own worth by whether or not she has a man. One of the essential elements in developing your worth is by having a healthy outlook on life and the ability to recognize that you don't need someone else to make you feel good about yourself.

✔ **Because you're tired of being alone.**

"Having a piece of man is better than having no man at all!" How many times have we heard this one? Being lonely can make a woman latch on to *any* man that shows interest in her out of desperation.

Ladies, it is okay to *not* have a man in your life! It is also possible to be *happy* and *single* at the same time. When you learn to relax and enjoy your single status, rather than running out and getting involved with the first available man that shows interest in you, you will be mentally and emotionally ready when that special man does come along.

✓ **Because all of your friends are either in a committed relationship or already married.**

Another common reason why women desire a long-term relationship or marriage is because all of her friends are doing it. The saying, "Always a bridesmaid, never a bride" does have an effect on some women.

Starting a relationship based on any of the reasons above can create a situation that is destined for disaster. If you find the need to be in a relationship for any of the reasons above, you may need to seek professional help in order to help identify the root of the real problem.

However, if you find that you are emotionally healthy enough to be in a relationship, then you must consider a few important factors.

It is of the utmost importance for a woman to understand what she is looking for in a man in order to know if she is pursuing the *right* man. That's right, ladies, you should be selective and choose wisely before rushing into any relation-ship or commitment.

Remember what I said in the introduction about our selection process? We must learn to make better choices when selecting a man to be in a relationship with. Part of that process is knowing what *you* want before you can determine if *he* is the one. After all, who wants to waste time, energy, and effort pursuing a man only to find out later that he's not the right one?

Being in a healthy, loving relationship is a wonderful feeling. Just knowing your special someone loves you unconditionally, in spite of all that you are, is enough to bring a smile to your lips. The man you choose to be in a relationship with should compliment your existence, not complete it. He should add to the experience of living, not take away from it or be the reason for it. He should celebrate the amazing woman that you are.

Committing to a long-term relationship or marriage comes with enormous responsibility and is a decision that shouldn't be taken lightly. You should look at committing to a relationship as you would purchasing a home. You have certain requirements that the home must meet before you enter into a contract on it. First, you establish that it has all of the features and amenities that you want. You make sure that it has the appropriate number of bedrooms and bathrooms. Maybe it has a pool or maybe it is the neighborhood that is the deciding factor for selecting that particular home. Whatever your reasons are, and because you could possibly be committed for an extended period of time, you want to make sure that the home meets your required specifications before you buy it.

When it comes to a relationship you should follow the same rules. Examine it. Get to know if it is something you want before becoming locked into a commitment for an extended amount of time. Make sure he has all the "amenities" you are looking for.

How many times have we heard women say that they married the wrong man? What makes a man the wrong man? Is it because he is incompatible with her? Is it their inability to communicate with each other?

Maybe these women didn't necessarily marry the wrong man, but maybe she didn't establish what her expectations were prior to committing to marriage. In many cases, she could have controlled the outcome of this failed relationship or marriage by using the process of elimination from the beginning to determine if the man was right for her. In many cases, marriages turn out badly because partners don't know what they are looking for. So, it is important to have some preset expectations.

In *I Need Therapy*, I discussed the importance of setting standards for the man you want in your life. I know many relationship experts discourage making lists of any kind pertaining to expectations within a relationship, but I feel it is necessary to establish guidelines when selecting a potential mate. However, you must realize that your list is a guide and you must be realistic with your expectations.

When I refer to making a list, I don't mean making a list of superficial requirements like he must be tall, good-looking, and earn a six-figure salary. I mean make a list of realistic expectations such as he must have similar values, beliefs, and goals as you, or he must have a strong belief in God. Once again, be realistic with your expectations.

It is also crucial for a woman to choose a partner who has something to contribute to the relationship other than sex. When you look at your relationship and realize that the only thing right about it is sex, then there is a problem. This usually occurs in cases where women become sexually involved with a man too early in the relationship. It is much easier to notice the things that you don't like about a man when sex has not been brought into the equation.

Sex has the ability to confuse a woman. Once you become sexually involved with a man it is much harder to see his less desirable characteristics. This is why it is so essential to get to know and learn a man's character before beginning a sexual relationship with him.

Ask the right questions! When you initially start dating someone you do have the right to know if he is seeing, dating, living with or sleeping with someone else, so don't be afraid to ask. Asking these essential questions will most often eliminate you from falling into the following category.

One reason why some women can't get a commitment of marriage is because her man is already married to someone else. I developed a very simple plan that I call the "Hands-Off Rule". The "Hands-Off Rule" simply means: Keep your hands off someone else's man. Simple, right?

For some reason, to many women, this seems to be a difficult rule to follow. I am not trying to be condescending when I talk about women dating married men. Truth be told, over the years I have had my share of relationships with married men as well. It took some time, but as I grew older, I realized married men contribute nothing positive to our existence. We may benefit financially, get a few bills paid, enjoy going out and being pampered by them, but ultimately, a married man has to go home, and you are left alone. If a woman is already suffering from low self-esteem issues, her self-esteem will surely plunge even lower in this situation.

If you are currently involved, or have ever been involved with a married man, you need to examine what your reasons are or were for dating him.

A married man knows he has to be creative when it comes to persuading a woman to cheat with him. After all, he already has one major strike against him because he is married. Most women automatically consider him unavailable because of this reason. However, in most cases, married men are charming and he knows he has to do something *extra* to draw you in. For him, it's like fishing. It is a challenge, so he asks himself, "What can I do to get this lady?"

Think about it like this, when you meet a man and he tells you that he is married, most of the time you are going to go into defense-mode, simply because you are not interested in becoming his woman on the side. The right thing to do in this situation is to politely say, "I'm not interested," and *mean* it.

However, some women allow themselves to be reeled in by this charming married man. He might say something like, "Just go out to dinner with me once. You'll see that I'm a really nice guy." You automatically think, *What harm could one dinner do?* You never even realize you are slowly being manipulated. He is reeling you in. At this point, you still think you are in control.

When he arrives to pick you up, he's looking good, smelling good and he is even thoughtful enough to come bearing gifts like roses, perfume, and maybe even jewelry. By doing this he hopes to show his appreciation that you have chosen to spend some of your valuable time with him.

Furthermore, he is attentive and chivalrous. He opens the car door and takes your hand as he escorts you to your destination. In the restaurant, he pulls out your chair for you and waits for you to be seated before he seats himself. During dinner, he is charming and compliments you to no end. Finally, he may talk about his marriage and how unhappy he is. He is appealing to your sympathy and continues to reel you in.

At the end of the night, you decide you had a great time and you would love to see him again. After all, it never hurts to have a new friend! After a few more dates, you find him even more charming and thoughtful. He continues to romance you, and finally, you give in to his wooing and sleep with him.

Ladies, you have just reached the point of no return. *It's a wrap!* He just pulled his catch (you) out of the water. At this point he no longer cares where the relationship goes, you know he's married and he has already slept with you. However, he will continue to make some nice gestures to stay in your good graces. The sex exceeded his expectations and he wants to keep you happy so he can continue to come back.

As the "other woman" it's just the opposite. You enjoy being charmed and pampered, and now that you have had sex with him, you want a place in his life. For the moment, you will settle for being second best, but eventually, number two is going to want the number one spot.

Most women are guilty of dating a married man at some point in their lives. I know I have been there. However, I had to make a commitment to stop dating unavailable men. Women must analyze their reasons for allowing themselves to be the other woman. The most common reason I hear is that they got to know him intimately before the affair began. This was also my excuse.

The last married man I dated had been married to his wife for thirty-six years. He was a regular customer at a casino where I worked. Every time he came to play, he would seek me out. He would sometimes spend my entire shift playing at my table; win or lose. Many times he would lose in excess of $10,000, but wouldn't get up and leave because he wanted to be in my presence. I knew from the beginning he was married, so I rejected his advances. He was always an overly generous man and tipped extremely well. The dealers loved him. I always say that table game dealers are like bartenders; patrons come, play, and tell you their life story. He was no exception. When he came to my game he frequently talked about how unhappy he was in his marriage. Over the course of a year I learned his life story.

He had married young. To get his wife initially into bed, he promised he would marry her afterward. However, instead of marrying her he left town to pursue work in another city. His father, after finding out through her parents about his promise to marry their daughter, confronted him and told him that a real man never promises to marry a lady and then leaves her. So he married her to fulfill his promise. After they married, he left town and returned to Chicago to work while she stayed in Mississippi. For thirty-six years they had mostly shared a long distance relationship. He felt this was the reason for their long marriage. Although they were married, they had never really lived together.

One year after meeting him, he asked me to meet him after work and for some reason I didn't say no as I usually did. Needless to say, over the next few weeks I was charmed, he wooed me and our relationship began. He was known as what the casino termed a "high roller," someone who spends large amounts of money. He would always say that our relationship could last as long as I wanted it to last. He would also tell me, "She doesn't want for anything and neither will you."

It wasn't the money that kept me there, because I was earning a comfortable salary. I owned my own home, drove a top of the line vehicle and I was paying my own bills. In addition, I was accustomed to being with men who had means, so I wasn't easily impressed by the material things that he gave me. But somehow he made quite an impression on me. Maybe it was the fact that although he lived three hours away, he would make the drive to come fix everything that needed repairing in my home. Maybe it was because he paid attention to detail and knew what need to be done without me ever having to ask. Initially, he would come into town and spend two days a week with me. As the relationship progressed, the time we spent together began to decrease. His wife was becoming suspicious, he had recently retired from his job, but he was still making frequent overnight trips out of town. I would get so frustrated at being left alone and felt that he wasn't giving me what I needed, namely, his time, so I began making demands.

Anytime I began threatening to date someone else, he would call me and tell me to go to Western Union to pick up some money. It was common for him to send me $2,500 to go shopping anytime he felt I was getting restless with the relationship. He would frequently say, "I'm giving you everything you could possibly need so you won't have to deal with the knuckleheads out there." Although he was financially generous, I had convinced myself that I didn't want the money anymore, I wanted the man. I didn't want to be the *other* woman; I wanted to be the *only* woman. He would tell me he wanted to divorce his wife and be with me, but if he did, he wouldn't have anything to offer me. He knew she would take everything.

One night, eight months into the relationship, I became violently ill. I was experiencing uncontrollable bouts of vomiting, sweating profusely and cramping. In my weakened state, I couldn't think clearly and I picked up the phone to call him. There was no answer, not that I expected there to be. Anytime he was in her presence he would send my calls to voicemail. I had alienated all of my friends because I was dating him. I didn't want to call 911 but I knew I couldn't drive myself to the hospital.

Still vomiting, and scrolling through the numbers in my phone, I happened across a male co-worker's number who had been interested in dating me for years. I had never shown him any attention other than to occasionally speak a polite hello and make some small talk, but he lived somewhere in the area, so I chanced calling him.

When my call connected to him, I could barely get out the words to tell him who I was in between bouts of vomiting. Yet he understood that it was me and I told him I needed to get to a hospital. Fortunately, he happened to be within two miles of my home at the time of my call. Being that he had never previously been to my home, I gave him directions and went outside so he could see me.

When he pulled into my driveway, I was lying on the ground. He helped me to his car and took me to the nearest hospital. As he was wheeling me into the hospital, I was still violently ill. They immediately put me into a room and gave me a shot to control the nausea. My friend, John, stayed with me and held a damp cloth to my forehead all night. I remember looking up at him and saying, "I bet you don't like me so much now, do you?" He replied, "Even as you were throwing up you are still the most beautiful woman I have ever seen."

I stayed at the hospital for nine hours, and when I was released, John took me home and left to go get ready for work. He was scheduled to be at work two hours after he dropped me off and he hadn't even been to sleep that night.

The following day, at my married lover's convenience, he called to see what my frantic message was about the previous night. When I told him about my ordeal he asked if everything was alright now. When I assured him that it was, he said, "Good! I'll call you back. My wife and I are having lunch and she's waiting for me." At that point, I realized that I would never be more than the "other" woman.

It took eight months and this major lesson for me to reach my breaking point. I considered myself fortunate because if I'd never developed this mild case of food poisoning, who knows how long I would have hung in there. At this point, I realized I deserved more than what I was getting and I didn't want him or his money anymore. So, I ended the relationship. Afterwards, I realized that I had disillusioned myself into thinking that I wanted this man to leave his wife, when in actuality I didn't. As the old saying goes, *we always want what we can't have.* For me, it was a challenge because I wanted him. But it was totally my fault, because I had opened my heart to love someone who was unavailable. For him, it was the excitement of being with someone who made him feel young and alive. He came to me for the excitement that he wasn't getting at home. And although he was financially making my life extremely comfortable by sending me major money, she was at home spending $10,000 on furniture for the home he had just built for them. Compared to what she had, I wasn't getting anything! While I was sitting at home alone on Valentine's Day with the $2,000 he'd sent me to buy myself a "nice" gift (as he called it), he was taking his entire family out to dinner.

Ladies, look at it this way. Why should you give your body to a married man while his wife gets all the glory?

True story, recently a friend called me to say that after two years of being fed up with being the other woman, she called her lover's wife and told her all about their affair. Her intention was to motivate the wife to divorce her cheating spouse. However, the wife's response was quite unexpected.

The wife said she knew about their affair from the beginning and she didn't care. She told her, "Every time he leaves you his guilty conscious eats him up, so he comes home and give me large sums of money to go shopping. So keep sleeping with his musty ass and soon I'll have put away enough money to leave his broke ass," she replied.

This young lady was heartbroken, but this is the reality of dating a married man. Married men come to you to make him feel young, sexy and wanted. However, he shares a history with his wife. She shares his life and knows his secrets. She has seen him at his worst where you have only seen the polished side of him.

Ladies, it is time to draw the line and make a commitment to stop dating unavailable men. Do not allow yourself to be the other woman. We have more control than we think in eliminating infidelity. If we raise our standards and refuse to demean ourselves by lying down with a man who is married, there would be far more successful, lasting relationships because it would drastically eliminate a man's options of finding a woman who will allow him to cheat. When you realize that you deserve to have all the benefits of a full, enriching relationship, it should be easy to avoid getting caught up.

For those of you who don't know who *is* off limits, a man is considered unavailable if he is married, in a relationship, living or sleeping with someone. Remember, married men contribute nothing positive to our existence. Recognize that a married man has people in his life who love and depend on him and he's not going to destroy that because of you.

I know right now, many of you who are or have been in a relationship with a married man are probably saying, "Well, I didn't know he was married!" Okay, maybe you didn't. But there is no excuse for *not* knowing. Take off those blinders, question strange behavior you don't understand (unexplained absences, unanswered phone calls, etc.) and stop making excuses. I know sometimes it is easy to cross paths with men who are good at hiding the fact that they are married, but this usually occurs when they no longer care about their marriage. When a man no longer cares about his marriage, he may frequently spend the night with you. He may be easily reached when you call his cell phone or office. He may indeed display behaviors of a man who is not married. However, here is another example and this next scenario is a bit extreme.

Recently, I spoke with a man who admitted that a lady he was interested in confessed to him that she had been with her previous man for two years and never knew he was married. It was his first time visiting her home and after hearing this, he said he got up from his seat and said, "It was nice meeting you, but I have to go." Just knowing that she could be so gullible made him question why he would ever be interested in her.

Ladies, there is no excuse for not knowing if your man is married. Whether we use it or not, ALL women are equipped with a built-in bullshit meter. The signs are always there. It's time to stop making excuses and stop sleeping with unavailable men. It's important to recognize that cheating causes heartache for everyone involved except for THE CHEATER! Do not allow yourself to be the other woman. Let's classy it up, ladies! Men who are married, dating, living with and/or sleeping with someone else should be OFF LIMITS!

As a woman, you already know what you can and cannot tolerate and only you know what you expect and need from your relationship, so take time and evaluate what those needs are before rushing into and committing to a relationship with someone who couldn't possibly love you.

Women should practice caution at the beginning of a new relationship when they don't really know a man well. Most of us are not wise when it comes to getting into a relationship. This is because initially, the attractiveness of a man can overshadow his faults. Sometimes those faults can be obvious, yet we still choose to overlook them.

The early stages of a relationship are when lasting impressions are formed, and this phase provides us the opportunity to take a clear-eyed look at a man who we may become involved with. However, realize that this is also when you will be scrutinized as well. Your first impression is what sets you apart from everyone else in the world. So, when meeting a man for the first time, it is to your advantage to make the best first impression possible, because men *do* judge us at our initial meeting, just as we judge them.

I am always amazed at how so many women don't understand the significance of first impressions. This holds true in any case, whether you are trying to get a job or a man. Good first impressions are paramount to our success in everyday life. It is easy to forget that everyone didn't grow up with the same lifestyle. Some people are not as privileged as others; nor have we all been exposed to the same situations in life. Which is another reason my writing is so important to me. I want women from all walks of life to know that they have all the tools available to them to change their lives for the better, so that they can achieve their goals. Every woman should be confident in her abilities to make the necessary changes in her life so that she is capable of achieving her dreams. It doesn't matter if you grew up in Beverly Hills or the ghetto. In this next scenario, I will show you how making necessary changes can literally change your personal *and* professional life.

Several years ago I met a young lady who worked at a local car wash. She had a three-year-old daughter and told me that her baby's father was not active in her daughter's life. She spent much of her time being depressed. She didn't enjoy working at the car wash for less than minimum wage, but since she dropped out of high school she felt she couldn't do any better. Appearance wise, she was straight ghetto. She grew up in the projects and her look displayed her upbringing. Her black hair was streaked with platinum blonde; she wore huge doorknob sized earrings and lots of colorful makeup.

Whenever I took my vehicle in to be detailed we would talk extensively. Over time, I learned she was quite an intelligent girl and had dreams of owning her own beauty salon. However, under her circumstances, she didn't feel she could do any better. I encouraged her to pursue her education and get her GED, and shortly thereafter, she did. When she received that certificate I was so proud of her that I took her out to dinner to celebrate her accomplishment. I'll never forget the look in her eyes as she thanked me for helping her make the first step. I continued to mentor her. She took my advice and started dressing the part of a professional. She later attended cosmetology school and now, a few years later, I'm proud to say that she has achieved her dream of opening her own salon.

All it took was setting a goal and taking the necessary steps to follow it through. If you desire to change how you live and rise above stereotypes of where you come from, all it takes is a little effort and planning. This young lady made a major transformation in her life. By making these changes, she increased her value, not only to herself and her daughter, but to a potential man as a partner. Her image changed from a girl who grew up in the projects, to one of a young lady that people could respect. In addition, she celebrated her second wedding anniversary a few months ago. Good first impressions are essential in your personal and professional life.

Building a successful relationship that ultimately leads to marriage begins with a solid foundation. It is essential to make a good first impression because it contributes to a foundation that is put in place at the initial meeting. Everything that happens from that point on is built on that one moment. Therefore, it is important to begin the construction of the relationship using genuine material such as honesty, integrity, trust and mutual respect. If not, at some point later on everything that was built using defective material will eventually fall apart.

Your genuine material cannot be lacking or substituted. You can't say, "Well, I don't have any nails, so I'm going to glue it together." Try gluing something together that should be nailed and see what happens. Sure, it might stick for a minute, but ultimately it will fall apart. Relationships are the same way. When you start it off right, it can withstand the elements and last a lifetime.

Even though it is important to make a good first impression, it is even more important to stay true to yourself as a person. Ladies, do not confuse this with what I said earlier. When you make certain changes in your appearance or the circumstances surrounding your life, you're not changing who you are as a human being, you are making changes that will improve your life as a whole.

When meeting someone you are interested in, never put any unnecessary pressure on yourself by starting that potential relationship under false pretenses. Do not lie, deceive, or pretend to be someone else in order to make yourself appear more than what you are. You want a person to like you for who you are, not for what they expect or want you to be. For example, do not tell a man you only have one child when you actually have five children. It may seem harmless at the moment, but what happens if you actually do get into a relationship?

This was a situation that actually happened to my friend Stephen. He was interviewing a young lady for a job and found himself very impressed by her. He boasted that she was the most beautiful young woman he had ever seen. After the interview, he hired her for a position in the company that he worked for. However, soon afterwards, they became involved in a romantic relationship which was so serious he asked her to move in with him. Everything was going well and they were having a blissful relationship. Steven enjoyed spending time with his girlfriend and her five-year-old daughter. A few months into the relationship, the company he worked for offered Stephen a promotion contingent on him relocating to another branch. This required Stephen to move to another city. Steven agreed to the move as long as his girlfriend was also given a transfer so they could continue to be together. The request was granted and Steven's girlfriend left her young daughter in the care of her mother until they were settled into their new home. On the weekends she would return home to visit with her daughter.

One particular weekend Stephen's schedule permitted him to accompany his girlfriend home. When they arrived, six small children ran out to the car to greet them enthusiastically yelling, "Mama's home!"

When Stephen asked his girlfriend, "Why are all these kids calling you mama?"

She responded, "These are my children. My mother has legal guardianship."

Stephen admitted to feeling shocked and overwhelmed. For the first time in their six month relationship he found out that she had not one, but six children. Of course, he ended the relationship, not because she had six children, but because she had not told the truth. She took away his choice as to whether or not he wanted to be with her and her six kids. This is why you should always be honest and upfront about your circumstances.

This principle applies to men as well as women. How many times have you met someone and when you initially got together they appeared to have it all together? However, months later, you find out that this person has misrepresented themselves. Well, it happens. When we meet someone that we are interested in, sometimes there is such a desperate need to impress that person. Someone might think that no one could possibly be interested in the person that they really are, so they lie to make themselves appear more worthy. Many times, they never realize if a relationship does develop the truth will eventually emerge. But some people never think beyond the initial meeting and it is easy to get caught up in the moment.

Usually, women begin to size a man up as marriage material from the initial meeting. In many cases, they are already fantasizing about the possibility of a future with this person, possibly even thinking up names for their first born child. However, most men do not think that way, and don't see beyond the initial meeting and a possible hook-up. They don't usually look at a woman and think, *Someday this could be my wife!* So some men (and women too) have been known to take this opportunity to fabricate the details of their life.

For example, a few months ago I received an email from a young lady who was extremely distraught. She had recently found out that her husband of three years, previously had served time in prison for rape. They had dated for two years before they were married, yet he never mentioned anything about serving time in prison. She found out about his prior record by accident when he was turned down for a job because of it. This young lady admitted to feeling hurt and betrayed because he never told her about this situation. For her, the hardest thing about the situation was accepting the fact that he had been convicted of rape. She admitted she would rather he had been convicted of murder. She also admitted that although all of this happened prior to him getting together with her, she didn't know if she could trust him anymore.

Communication and trust are two of the most valuable elements in a relationship. When we live in close proximity with another person there will always be differences of opinions. However, it is when these differences are not discussed that confusion and conflict arise.

This young lady was clearly angry because her husband withheld important information about his past; therefore, he breached her trust in him. No relationship can exist without trust! For a woman, trust exists when she is secure in her relationship, when she knows she can depend on her partner to protect and not hurt her. This young lady was hurt, and as a result, she didn't know what to do about her discovery. She was torn as to whether she should leave him, because trust had been breached, or if she should stay with her husband in order to make the commitment work. Regardless, her new reality was that she was married to a convicted rapist.

She wanted me to help her make a decision, but I explained to her that I could not do that because I don't know her husband or his character. No one could make that decision for her but her. However, I did ask her one critical question. "Did you trust him before finding out about his past?" She admitted that she did. I also asked, "Was he a good husband and provider before you found out about his past?"

She replied, "Without a doubt!"

I understood the feelings of hurt and betrayal, because in some of my previous relationships I have had similar experiences and disappointments. In this case, her husband claimed he never mentioned his past because he feared if he had disclosed this bit of information at the beginning of the relationship, she probably wouldn't have gotten involved with him.

This is the primary reason most men (and women too) won't disclose any information if he feels the information in question will hurt his chances with you. Although this may be true, and it could possibly ruin any chance of there being a relationship, it is always best to be honest and let the other party decide for themselves if they want to become involved with you.

Remember, very few people have a past that is squeaky clean. If you have concerns that a person will leave you because of your past, don't think withholding information will stop them from leaving once the truth is finally revealed. Betrayal of any kind hurts. When you withhold information the situation doesn't change, only the timing changes. So, if your partner might have left you initially upon finding out the truth about you, after finding that you have intentionally withheld important information, they may still leave. It doesn't matter how long you've kept the secret. If a person cannot accept you for the person that you are in spite of your past, then take it with a grain of salt and move on.

As I said earlier, men do judge women based on the initial meeting and you can sabotage a potential relationship by revealing too much too soon. The number one mistake many women make on a first date (other than having sex with him, but we'll address that later) is getting too personal and revealing too much information.

When you meet someone you are interested in, it is normal to want to rush the relationship by revealing as much about yourself as possible. However, getting to know someone happens in stages, so take your time and let it develop naturally before you start revealing your entire life history. Look at your first date as a getting to know each other period. In order to make it to the next date, it has to be an enjoyable experience for the both of you.

Most men do not like drama, so it would be wise to figure out if there is a possibility of a relationship before you start unloading your excess baggage on him. As I said earlier, the proper way to deal with this situation is to already have checked your baggage at the door, so that you are not dragging it with you into your potential new relationship.

Therefore, if your ex-boyfriend (or for you men, ex-girlfriend) beat you so badly that you were in the hospital for weeks, the first date is *not* the time to discuss it, as it could make him wonder what did *you* do to provoke your ex. Even though you may have been perfectly innocent in this situation and did nothing to provoke the abuse, we have a habit of sympathizing with our gender.

For example, if a man tells a woman that his ex-girlfriend dumped him, the first thing she thinks is what did he do to cause it?

Do not misinterpret what I am saying by thinking I'm making light of this situation. Abuse of any kind is a serious matter and is unacceptable regardless of the circumstances. In my past, I have experienced many forms of abuse. Even so, the first date is not the time to discuss it. The first date is not the time to discuss "any" past relationships, after all, who really cares if your ex cheated on you with your sister? Your potential interest does not need to hear about it when he is focused on getting to know you. It is best not to discuss anything that will distract your potential interest or give him cause to not schedule the next date.

Ladies, this situation is a Catch 22. You want to be open and honest, but there is a fine line between what you should disclose on a first date and what you should wait to reveal until you have determined if the relationship is going somewhere. In addition, there are certain key things that you should ask of him and should disclose about yourself on the first date. The best way to explain what I'm talking about is to tell you about this experience.

Quite some time ago, I met a man while on a job in an Air Force Base Commissary. The chemistry between us was obvious and we talked briefly before he asked for my number. I told him I didn't feel comfortable giving him my number, but that I would look forward to seeing him when he made his next visit into the store. When he left, I was practically kicking my own butt because I was attracted to the man, and I did want to see him again. Now I had to wait until his next visit to give him my number (if there was a next visit).

Fortunately, I looked up a few days later and there he was. This time, as he came through my line he exclaimed that he only came back to see me. I gave him my number and he called me the following day.

During our first phone conversation I asked him my "need to know" questions, including: "Are you married, dating, living with or sleeping with someone?" Initially, he hesitated. He was more than likely thinking about how to answer this question (this was the first red flag). But his hesitation gave me my answer. After thinking about it, he replied, "Well, technically I'm still married, but I have been separated from my wife for four years. We are in the process of getting divorced, but every time it comes down to our final court date something changes." He assured me that the divorce papers had been filed and he was more than willing to let me take a look at them. I declined as I felt this was totally unnecessary.

During the entire conversation he never asked me any-thing about myself. Not my age, if I had children or even if I was currently dating anyone (second red flag). He didn't ask because that would leave an opening for me to ask him those same questions. However, I wanted to know, so I asked if he had children. He told me that he has three, all by his soon-to-be ex-wife. *Hmm… no outside children,* that was impressive, I thought. Then I asked their ages. Again, he attempted to sidestep the question by saying (red flag number three), he likes to reveal certain information about himself as a relation-ship progresses, not everything up front. However, I was not taking his response for an answer and pressed on. Ultimately, he told me his children's ages, ten, six and… *four months!* Let's do the math, ladies. He's been separated from his wife for four years, he's forty-nine-years-old with a four month old baby. *Whew!* Talk about some baggage! But I wasn't ready to discredit him, YET!

The next day he called and asked if I would like to go to a movie. Although I had some doubts, I was still interested in him, so I accepted. Since it was our first date I agreed to meet him at the theatre. It is always a good idea to arrange your own transportation when you don't know someone very well and you are not ready for them to pick you up at your home. Always offer to meet him at the location.

We met half an hour before the movie was scheduled to start, which allowed us some time to talk. There was no denying that he was attractive and I found myself asking, "Tell me again why you're not dating anyone?"

He looked away and said, "Well, that's one of those things that I wanted to discuss with you in person. I'm kind of seeing someone, but she doesn't live here in town. I was going to tell you about that after the movie." (red flag number four; baggage, baggage and more BAGGAGE!)

I said to him, "When we spoke on the phone, I asked you very direct questions and you only told me about your estranged wife. You never spoke of a girlfriend!" He apologized and said he did not realize until after we ended our conversation that he hadn't told me the whole story. (Yeah, right!) But you know what, ladies? I kept it classy! Since he had already purchased the tickets to the show we saw the movie. Afterwards, I thanked him, told him that I enjoyed the show and his company but felt he had some issues in his life that I did not want to be a part of and if I continued to see him I would be going against everything that I believed in. Then I went home.

I'm sure most of you have encountered men who were less than honest about their situations. I shared this so that you will see it is up to you to hold a man accountable for his actions. Do not let anyone slip anything past you, because if you allow it, he will do it. His intentions were to reel me in, thinking I would be so impressed by him I would overlook how he was misrepresenting himself.

Remember what I said earlier, always be honest about who you are. Also, do not discuss your desire to get married and start a family on a first date. Men view women who discuss marriage when they first meet as desperate and needy. He may think that instead of really trying to get to know him you are just husband hunting. This will surely drive him away, because at that moment, all he is interested in is getting to know you and having a good time.

When you meet a man who has aroused your interest, draw him in with your wit and charm. Give off positive vibes.

Never speak badly about other men. If you do, it may be perceived that you are bitter and that you may have a problem with men in general. Keep your potential interest intrigued by being your warm, charming, sensual self. At the same time, be cautious of how you portray yourself in public. The way you present yourself makes an enormous difference in how men respond to you. So be aware of the signals you may be sending out.

For example, you desire to be in a long-term committed relationship, but while in the club or bar you meet a guy that you are developing a connection with on the dance floor. You decide to take him home and have sex with him on the first night. Now here you are weeks later wondering why he hasn't called as he said he would. You keep going back to the same club just hoping you will run into him again.

Ladies, we must stop making it so easy for men to use us. When you meet a man that you are interested in, do not immediately jump into bed with him. Give yourself time to see if you still want him *after* the alcohol wears off. Although it is possible to develop a long-term relationship with someone you just met and had sex with on the first night, chances are nothing serious will result from it. If you allow a man to have sex with you on the same night that you meet him, you better believe he is wondering how many other men you've met and gave it up to on the first night—especially if you met him in a club or a bar.

Remember my most important rule: *"Allow a man time to get into your head and heart before allowing him into your body."* Take some time and really listen to the things he is telling you. The more you listen, the more you learn what type of man he really is. Learning the truth about a man can help you stop being hurt by someone who couldn't possibly love you. We have more control in potential relationships than we think. It is up to you to set the tone of the relationship from the onset. Remember, *it is much easier to make a good first impression than it is to erase a bad first impression.*

It is important to give a man time to develop romantic feelings for you before you become involved in a sexual relationship. Make a potential mate *earn* your goodies. You should never just hand it over to him.

Successful relationships are built on trust. When you initially meet a man you don't know who he is. So never trust anyone until you learn their true character. Learning a person's character comes with time. Look at it this way, you wouldn't turn over the keys to your brand-new car to a man you do not know, would you? I have a hard enough time giving the keys to my vehicle to someone I do know, but giving them to a complete stranger is out of the question. You wouldn't give the keys to your home to a total stranger and invite him to come on in and make himself at home. So why would you give up your most prized possession and most valuable asset to someone if you don't know his true character?

I always say that having sex too early in the relationship is like committing relationship suicide. You have to give yourself time to develop a connection and allow the excitement to build. There are too many things that could go wrong when you allow sex too early in a relationship.

From a woman's perspective, a man may have a number of visible faults that are magnified when we become sexually involved too soon. He may have a small penis, and we already know how overly critical women are of men who have small penises, or he may experience premature ejaculation due to over-excitement. I'm not saying this to be funny, but I hear from women all the time that had sex with a man upon meeting him and the experience turned her off so badly she felt getting involved in a relationship with him might prove to be too much work. Granted, both problems could still exist even if you give yourself time to get to know him; he may still be a premature ejaculator or have a small penis, but the difference is, after allowing yourself the opportunity to get to know him you are more likely to continue with the relationship because you have already developed that emotional connection with him.

From a man's perspective, although sex with you may have been good sex, he may lose interest simply because now he knows he does not have to have a relationship with you in order to have sex with you. He may still want to have sex with you, but he probably won't want a relationship with you. Most men will weigh the fact that you didn't make him wait for it, you didn't allow enough time to make him really want it, and you definitely didn't make him work for it. Men usually don't have sex first, then look forward to getting to know you afterwards. The steps are in the reverse order. He wants to get to know you in order to have sex with you. So when you give him the sex first, what else is there to look forward to?

By giving yourself time to get to know each other it protects you both. Having sex too early in the relationship has the ability to leave you with this empty, unfulfilled feeling and can make you ask yourself, "Now what?" In some of my previous encounters where I allowed sex too soon, I felt that he enjoyed it more than I did. In some cases, after it was over, in my disappointed state, I only wanted to rush him out of my home because it was so awkward and uncomfortable as he tried to explain it would be better the *next* time. In some cases, there was no next time because I wasn't willing to give him a second opportunity.

In recent years, I have developed a new awareness about sex that I didn't have as a younger adult. I have a different approach about sex now. For me, sex comes with love and that factor is a prerequisite for sex. I absolutely must have time to develop romantic, loving feelings before I commit my body.

Sex alone cannot sustain a relationship. When I am truly interested in a man, I don't mind letting him know that I prefer to wait simply because if we have sex before I develop genuine feelings for him, we may not live up to each other's expectations and the relationship could be over before it ever begins. If he cannot deal with that, it is best that I know up front. If he doesn't agree, he has to find someone else who is willing to give him what he wants.

When you give yourself time to get to know someone before engaging in sexual intercourse it becomes more than just about copulation. In the context of a relationship, sex is a beautiful thing. When you give yourself to a man out of love, it takes on a deeper and more fulfilling meaning. Your sexual experience becomes an ethereal, almost spiritual connection. Ladies, if you have ever experienced this, then you know what I'm talking about, and if you haven't been there with a man, then you should desire to do so.

So, it is always best to give yourself time to get to know a man before beginning a sexual relationship with him. Sex has proper timing in a relationship and all the required factors have to be in place in order for a relationship to flourish.

Remember: *Allow a man time to get into your head and your heart before you allow him into your body!* Following my most important rule can help prevent you from a whole lot of heartache and disappointment. We all know that any woman can find a man to sleep with her, but on the other hand, if a man will have sex with you – and not think of you as marriage material – it says a lot about how he perceives you.

Remember, men are more selective when choosing a woman for a long-term commitment or marriage, than they are when choosing a sexual partner. And only you can determine which one you will be.

Don't let your first date with a man take place at your home or his. Do not allow yourself to be enticed with the invitation of a home-cooked dinner prepared by him. Yeah, I know it sounds inviting, but if he cannot take you out then pass on seeing him altogether.

Men tend to think of the first date as being expensive. He already knows that you expect him to impress you, so he knows he will have to spend some money. However, since he doesn't know if you are worth it, he may opt for an at-home movie night and takeout pizza, which will give him an opportunity to feel you out without making a dent in his wallet.

Chances are if you allow him into your home before he ever takes you out, you run the risk of falling into a sexual relationship sooner than you intended. This situation is a no-no for many reasons. You are already sexually attracted to each other and under the right circumstances, it is bound to get physical. It might start out simple; kissing, touching, a caress here and there, and then one thing leads to another, then before you know it...sex happens! Ladies, do not put yourself in a situation that you may not be ready for.

Okay, now let's just say that it happened. You got caught up and ended up sleeping with him sooner than you planned. It's okay, don't freak out. Whatever you do, do not turn into an after-sex stalker. An after-sex stalker tries to overcompensate for allowing sex too soon by constantly ringing his phone off the hook, texting every few minutes, and stalking his social media sites wanting to know when the two of you will be getting together again.

Ladies, the best thing you can do in this situation is to back the hell off! Give him some time to absorb what has happened. At this point, the best thing you can do is to let him make up his mind if he wants to pursue a relationship with you. Women immediately equate sex with love. After sex, you immediately expect a man to want a relationship. Keep in mind, men do not think this way.

So, let's say the damage has been done. Now let's address some ways that we can fix this situation. If the man of your interest calls you within a couple of days, it's all good. You can still turn this negative experience into a positive one, but for the sake of argument, let's just say he calls, but instead of asking you out, he wants to get together again for sex. This is your opportunity to tell him that although you enjoyed sex with him, you are not looking for a casual sex partner, and it seems that the "relationship" is starting to be just about sex, and you want more than that from him. You just placed the ball in his court. You have just made him aware that he cannot have just a sexual relationship with you, so now *he* has to make a decision.

Don't be disappointed if the decision he makes is not the one you want. There is always the possibility that he won't make any other attempts to call or see you again. Men are funny that way and he could be thinking any number of things. As I said earlier, maybe he feels he doesn't have to have a relationship with you now because he's already had the sex. Who knows what could be on his mind. Whatever happens from this point on, you have to be okay with it. Use it as a learning experience. Do not make the same mistake in your future relationships.

Remember: *There is nothing wrong with playing yourself as long as you learn something from it.*

Some women have problems understanding their role in a relationship. I receive countless emails in which women express to me the need to know where they stand in their relationships. These women expect their man to clarify if they are actually in a relationship or if he is just using her for sex. Ladies, let me assure you that if you have to ask someone other than your man what your role is with him, you should already know that you are not "in a relationship."

Women need to check a man's actions in order to determine where she stands with him. Sure, it might be the right thing for him to tell you where you stand, but it is not always necessary for him to verbally acknowledge to you whether or not he is in a relationship with you.

A man's actions will tell you where you stand quicker than any words that could ever come out of his mouth. Pay attention to warning signs because they are always there. Never try to rationalize or make excuses for your man's bad behavior. Does he take you out and spend quality time with you, or does he only see you when he comes by late at night looking for sex?

If a man spends his social hours hanging out with his buddies or doing whatever else he chooses to do and only comes by to spend time with you afterwards, you are just a casual sexual partner, a jump off, booty call, or whatever other terminology you may be familiar with.

One woman told me she had been seeing her man off and on for over nine months, yet she had never been to his home. How is this possible? He managed to keep her away from his home by using the excuse that as a single parent, he wasn't ready for his kids to meet her yet. Seriously?!

Ladies, when you are involved in situations such as this you should already know that you are not in a relationship. You need to figure out why this man continues to see you. Then you need to figure out why you are allowing it. You may have to ask yourself, "What is he getting from the relationship?" Usually, it's sex, but some women are known to buy expensive gifts and give money to a man hoping that this will inspire him to want to be with her. Next, ask yourself, "What am I getting from it?" What does this man contribute to you and your well-being that you cannot provide for yourself?

Ladies, you don't have to settle for being just a booty call. You have so much to offer to a man who is worthy. If you continue to allow men to walk into your life and devalue you, he will continue to do so, as long as you allow it.

Men love and respect women who first show love and respect for themselves!

If you are the type of woman who allows this type of behavior, you can't even get his time, so you already know that you will not be receiving a marriage proposal. And why would you want a proposal from someone who treats you so callously anyway? Think about it!

Some women find themselves falling into a "friends-with-benefits" relationship with a man she may be attracted to. In many cases, some men won't tell a woman who shows interest in him that he is not looking for a commitment, but he will allow a friends-with-benefits relationship. There is nothing wrong with a friends-with-benefits relationship as long as each party knows where they stand and as long as they can keep it in perspective. Ladies, I'm saying there is nothing wrong with this arrangement *if* you are not looking for a long-term commitment or marriage. However, some women will initially agree or allow this arrangement, either by admission or by action, but as the relationship progresses, she will want to change the terms of the original agreement. Personally, I don't think friends-with-benefits relationships are healthy, simply because it is harder for a woman to maintain this type of relationship without her feelings getting involved. Once involved in a sexual relationship, women have a hard time differentiating between love and sex so women are more likely to confuse sex with love, and once a woman convinces herself that she is in love, it is almost impossible to convince her otherwise. But keep in mind, most men will want to continue with the original agreement as it leaves him free of commitment.

A twenty-two year old woman emailed me with her problem. She recently allowed a man she had been having a friends-with-benefits relationship with for two months to move into her apartment. By allowing him to move in she felt he would eventually want to be in a committed relationship with her. However, after he moved in he started slacking. When it came time to pay the bills he would always have an excuse as to why he didn't have his share. As a result, she found herself covering all of the living expenses.

Recently, this friend-with-benefits/roommate began bringing other women into their apartment. Although she knew they had no commitment to each other, she felt hurt when she had to listen to him having sex with another woman in her home. When she tried to talk to him about how this situation made her feel, he replied that since they shared the apartment he had every right to bring his women home. He even jokingly invited her to join in his sexual encounters.

This young lady clearly started the relationship in an inappropriate manner. She made several mistakes, she became involved in a friends-with-benefits relationship, she allowed him to move into her home, she allowed herself to be taken advantage of financially—and finally—she didn't put her foot down when she was being disrespected. As a result, she placed herself in a position that she could have easily avoided had she taken the time and thoroughly evaluated the situation rationally before allowing the problem to escalate to this point. This is why it is so important to establish expectations from a relationship before you fall into a situation that you may suffer repercussions for later.

Remember, whatever image you project to a man is exactly what you will get back. If it is negativity that you project, then that is what you will receive in return. There is a negative stigma attached to women about how we relate to our men and relationships. We are known to bitch, nag, and make unnecessary demands of our men. Unfortunately, this has become part of a woman's negative self-image, especially women of color. Women look to other women to corroborate in their negative opinions about men. Don't deny it, we do. Women get together, throw male-bashing parties and talk about all the things that the men in their lives are doing wrong. What women don't realize is that by participating in this, what they are actually doing is further contributing to the degradation of the image of the man in their life. And those women who corroborate those negative viewpoints are reinforcing those opinions, simply because most women have had some negative experiences with men and relationships.

Just because you have been through some negative relationships does not mean that the men you were involved with were bad people. When a man does something that disappoints you it doesn't make him a bad individual. Maybe he made some bad choices, but it doesn't necessarily mean he is a bad person.

I'm sure you've heard the term 'speak it into existence'. Well, this works for negativity just as it does positivity. If you think your man is lazy and no-good when you say it enough, in your mind, he really is!

This is why it is so important for women to develop a new attitude. If there is something you are unhappy with in your relationship, you have the ability to change it. You can also transform the man in your life by changing how *you* think. However, in order to start the process and transform your way of thinking, you must first change your attitude.

Throw that negative thinking out the window and project a new positive image starting today. Stop complicating the small things and spend some time trying to discover new ways to communicate your needs to your man. I assure you, your relationship will start to take an immediate drastic change.

✓ **Recognize your power.**

Most women don't recognize the power that they possess in a relationship. Women control most of the power in a relationship because nothing can really happen until we allow it to happen. Think about it. A relationship can't develop until a woman allows it to develop.

Some men admit that they recognize the powerful position women hold in a relationship, but they also know that some women lack the self-confidence and self-assurance to assert themselves. This makes them an easy target to be used and mistreated.

Subsequently, in many ways men are no different than women. Some men have been hurt so badly and taken advantage of until it's difficult for them to open up and trust a woman. Recognize that hurt works both ways and you are not the only one who has been through it. Recognizing your power also includes having the ability to make decisions about what is best for you in your relationships, whether you are just getting into it or if you have been in it for years.

When *I Need Therapy* was first released, a former co-worker purchased my book. A few days after she bought the book she approached me in the hallway at work and gave me the biggest hug. I was shocked because this was someone who had never said more than a polite hello during the entire four years we worked together. She told me that reading my book was one of the greatest experiences in her life, and then she shared a bit of her story with me. Two years prior, her husband of twenty-six years walked out on her. At the time, they were building a new home. A few days prior to the move, she returned home to find that her husband had moved all of his things but had left hers. When she called his cell phone to ask why he'd only moved some of their household items, he told her he had moved into their new home and he wanted a divorce. She was devastated. As it happened, her husband moved a younger woman into the home that he had originally built for his wife.

Her self-esteem was so damaged she couldn't get over it. She admitted to having frequent breakdowns at work. She would suddenly start crying with no warning and not be able to stop. Some days she was so depressed she couldn't bring herself to get out of bed. On top of it, she had been seeing a therapist for the entire two years since the divorce. We exchanged numbers and that was the beginning of our friendship.

She said reading my book touched something in her spirit and was responsible for the changes she ultimately made in her life. The lifeless person I was accustomed to seeing at work was now a beautiful, vibrant woman. She had a new attitude and a new outlook on life. She took control of her life and against my advice she decided to stop seeing her therapist. She felt she didn't need her anymore.

That was two years ago, we are now the best of friends and I haven't seen her depressed a day since.

✓ **Overcoming your self-esteem issues.**

Being a woman comes with tremendous responsibility. We are expected to be many things to many people. We take care of our children, our home, and our man, and in many cases, still manage to work a full-time job. All of those tasks are an enormous responsibility. Although it can be quite challenging to fit everything in, sometimes we have to handle it all on our own. It is unreasonable to think that we can take care of the people around us effectively if we neglect ourselves. If we did, we wouldn't be in any shape to take care of anyone else.

Women are emotional creatures, and many times our challenges in life can sometimes become too heavy to bear and we end up suffering feelings of inadequacy. In a world where everything is always changing, it can be difficult to keep up. Most women suffer from low self-esteem at some point in their lives. It doesn't matter who you are or what your circumstances in life may be. Some of the most beautiful women in the world suffer from low self-esteem. It doesn't matter your income level, or your social or economic background; most women experience self-esteem issues at some point. However, many times women will sabotage themselves and contribute to their own feelings of inadequacy. For example, a man pays his woman a compliment by telling her that she looks beautiful. Before the words leave his mouth, she chimes right in and says, "No I don't! I need a manicure and my hair needs a perm. See, look at my roots!"

Don't act like you don't know what I'm talking about, we have all done it, including me. This is what I call *self*-sabotage. We will take the time to point out our flaws, although most of the time, nobody ever notices these things until we point them out. Talk about self-sabotage! These insecurities are preventing women from living life to their fullest. For some women overcoming self-esteem issues can be difficult, but it is important to note that it is not impossible.

The first step to overcoming insecurity and gaining confidence is to surround yourself with positive energy. Oftentimes, it is the factors around you that contribute to your state of mind, so it is conducive to take the necessary precautions to change your mindset *and* your environment. Sometimes, in order to change you, you have to change your surroundings.

It is harder to overcome self-esteem issues when you are with someone who wants you to feel down about yourself. Many times, it is those closest to you that have the ability to hurt you the most by planting seeds of doubt in your mind. Even though you have love for the person you choose to be in a relationship with, when that person—who claims to love you—bears you ill will, you have to make some changes. If you are with someone who is overly critical and never has anything good to say to you or about you, you may need to reevaluate your relationship.

In order to feel good about yourself, you've got to have confidence, and you cannot be confident when someone is constantly putting you down. In order to grow, you have to surround yourself with positive people who genuinely love you.

Negativity breeds negativity. Have you ever met someone who could complain about anything? If it's sunny, it's too bright. When it's raining they want it to be sunny. Some people can complain about anything, and there are some people that you cannot satisfy, I don't care what you do. But if you are around someone who never has anything good to say about life or about you, your self-esteem will always suffer.

As I said earlier, there are many things that can be done to boost your level of self-confidence. So think about the things that make you feel good. I always feel my best when I am pampering myself because those special things that I do for me contribute to my well-being. There are many luxuries that I enjoy. I may indulge in a bubble bath with a good book and a glass of wine. I enjoy scented candles, so I surround myself with them. They smell yummy and make me feel yummy inside.

Also, when I'm lounging at home, I love to wrap myself in silky, sexy attire. There is something about the feel of silk against my skin that makes me feel ultra sexy.

When you feel good about who you are on the inside, you can't help but radiate that on the outside. The point is to do whatever it takes to make you feel good about yourself. So what if you haven't found your Mr. Right yet. You don't need a man in your life to experience love.

Learn to have a love affair with yourself. A spa day is a great way to pamper yourself. Treat yourself to a massage, get a complete makeover; including hair and nails. Go shopping, buy a new wardrobe. If you can afford it, consider going all out and indulge yourself in a big way by taking a trip to that exotic island you've been dreaming about. This could be the perfect opportunity to get your girlfriends together for a singles cruise. Join a gym. Working out conditions not only the body, but the mind, and it is a great way to relieve stress. When you are physically fit not only does it improve your overall health and well-being—by making you stronger and healthier—but your overall appearance improves. Being physically fit also assists in overcoming self-esteem issues.

It is a known fact that when you feel good, you look good. And as an added bonus, if you haven't already found your Mr. Right, the gym is an excellent place to meet single, successful, attractive men!

Part of loving yourself is surrounding yourself with people who love and care about you. Get your emotional self together by eliminating the negativity from your life. Keep in mind that this also includes the people that you care about most. Develop a plan, set some goals, and do whatever it takes to implement those goals. Remember the saying "A journey of a thousand miles begins with a single step." So don't worry if it doesn't happen overnight. Even if you find yourself taking baby steps, as long as you're moving forward you are doing great.

If you have someone in your life who is constantly telling you why you can't do anything or why you will never have anything, you have to cut them loose! If you have someone in your life that is stunting your growth, let them go. In order for there to be growth in your life, sometimes you have to step outside of your comfort zone.

✓ **Develop a positive self-image.**

Women have a tendency to sabotage their own self-image with negative thinking. No one is perfect and the sooner you realize that you don't *have* to be perfect, the sooner you will begin to accept the person you are. Recognize your worth and all that you have to offer to a man and a potential relationship. Make a list of all the things that make up the fabulous person that you are. Later, we will go into more detail about developing a positive self-image in a chapter titled *Why Should He Choose You?*

✓ **Recognize your worth!**

What is worth? When we think of worth, we automatically think of value, quality, character, or significance, just to name a few. So now, I want you to think of these words and apply them to you. What is your value, quality, character and significance? If someone asked, what would you say? Identify what makes you unique. What makes you special? What is your contribution, not just to your relationship, but to the world? Recognizing your abilities and accomplishments contribute to self-confidence, so don't be shy about revealing who you are.

✓ **Liberate yourself!**

Liberation is being free to make your own choices and decisions about where you want to be in life. The only thing holding you back is you!

✓ **Transform your attitude.**

There is a famous quote by William James, which states, "The greatest discovery of any generation is that a human being can alter his life by altering his attitude!" Your attitude determines the outcome of everything that happens in your life. If you don't have a positive attitude you will never achieve your goals. Sometimes having a positive attitude doesn't just happen. We have to make a conscious effort to make it happen. As I said before, women are blessed with the inherent ability to transform their lives. If there is anything you don't like about your life, do something to change it! It's just that simple.

✓ **Accept responsibility! Don't place the blame on a man for the things that we do to ourselves.**

Women play themselves all the time, then they are quick to blame a man for the things that he is doing (or has done). However, the fact might be that he didn't do anything other than what we allowed him to do. We would rather point the finger at him for the poor choices that *we* made. And it's okay. When you mess up, you have to blame someone, and it is a whole lot easier to blame someone else rather than to blame yourself. There is nothing wrong with slipping up and playing yourself as long as you learn something from it.

When I was younger, I played myself many times and in many situations. Then I would sit back and cry (like most women) about what *he* did to me. One of my reasons for writing this book is to teach women to make better choices. What does this have to do with getting your man to put that ring on your finger in 365 days or less? You see, we control our destiny, and we can get what we want when we start using our heads and common sense to make educated choices in our lives. I can cite many instances of how women play themselves, but let me tell you about a personal example of my own.

When I was twenty-three years old, and still new to the military, I was sent overseas to Korea. There I met Kevin Lewis, we called him Lew, and he was one of the finest men

I'd ever seen in my life. This man was what I call "bite-your-lip fine." You know the type, when he comes around you have to bite your lip to keep from saying something really stupid.

When you are in the military serving overseas, it's as if you're in your own little world. You know that the people you come in contact with have their own lives back in the States, just like you do. But over there, it's as if you're isolated from the rest of the world, and it is somewhat easier to act out your fantasies in a world where nobody really knows you.

Well, somehow I fell head over heels for Lew (or so I thought). Not only was he sexy as hell, but this man could get within ten feet of me and my body would react all on its own. Just seeing him walk into a room was enough to make me jumpy and jittery. Obviously, Lew knew the effect he had on me, and somehow, shortly thereafter, our illicit and torrid affair began. I can't refer to it as a relationship because we didn't date or go out anywhere in public. The times we were together was spent in either the privacy of my room or his.

We lived in a co-ed barrack, and although his room was on another floor, we resided in the same building, which was convenient. Much to my dismay, I soon discovered that Lew was messing around with me *and* this girl Patrice, whose room was a few doors down the hall from mine.

I remember the first time I discovered Lew was seeing her. I got up earlier than usual one morning to go take a shower, and as I was coming out of my room, he was sneaking out of hers. Judging from the expression on his face, he never expected to see me walking down the hall at that time of morning. I was furious, but instead of saying anything to him, I dropped my head as we passed each other in the hall and pretended that I didn't see him. I remember going into the bathroom and spewing obscenities. I called him every no-good cheating, son-of-a-bitch, under the sun. I spoke badly about him to my girlfriends, yet, I continued to have sex with him. I couldn't understand. What wasn't I giving him sexually that would make him want to cheat on me? And with *her* of all people. For the life of me, I couldn't understand what he saw in her. I must have gone through every scenario in my head trying to figure it out. She wasn't nearly as pretty as me. Yeah, I was vain, but she had this awful blotchy skin that was covered in acne. Although I felt I was prettier, I had to admit she had a better body. But that didn't excuse his cheating!

This went on for months. I never said anything to Lew about his relationship with Patrice. I never confronted him. And although there were many other times I caught him exiting her room before dawn, I still didn't say anything to him. I chose not to confront Lew because I knew if I did I was going to have to make a decision. Ironically, Patrice also caught him coming out of my room a few times and *she* ignored it, too. On those occasions, when she and I ran into each other in the shower, restroom, or in the hallway we would give each other that look. You know, that "bitch, please" look, but we never said anything to each other. Lew was transferred back to the States about six months later.

I look back now and laugh at how silly my thought process was at age twenty-three, but at that time, it was an enormous-ly stressful time in my life. I later realized that although I wasn't in love with Lew, I was addicted to what he was doing to me sexually. Therefore, I didn't want to rock the boat by saying anything that could possibly cause me to lose him. And I guess Patrice felt the same way.

Ultimately, I got smarter. I learned that I was using my sexual relationship with Lew to fill a void. I was addicted to what he was doing to me because of my own insecurities. Lew was good-looking, sexy, attractive, and *all* the women wanted him. But he selected me (as well as Patrice and possibly a few others) and in some warped way, this made me feel worthy. I was suffering from low self-esteem even though I didn't recognize it at the time. But Lew recognized it instantly, and I confirmed that for him when I dropped my head and pretended that I didn't notice him as he was sneaking out of this other woman's room.

Ladies, when you are insecure men can spot it from a mile away, and some men prey on women who display such weaknesses. If you are honest with yourself, when you meet someone new, it is relatively easy to determine who is sincere and who is not. You can usually tell if he genuinely desires to get to know you or if he only wants to have sex with you. Now when I meet someone I am attracted to, I look at the entire picture. I will observe not only his appearance but how he relates to me. I take note of the things that he is interested in and where his conversation goes. You can tell a lot about a man by what he says. For example, does he ask for your number or give you his? Does he add any stipulations on when is not a good time to call? And what are the reasons for those stipulations?

When I meet someone that I'm interested in, I have a responsibility to look out for me first, as nobody else is going to do that for me. If I give a man my number and the first contact I get is a text, I already know what's up. If he makes a habit of texting, but not calling, that's a problem. So, I draw the line, and I don't allow it to proceed any further.

I have a problem with texting because it is so impersonal. I feel that if a man is genuinely interested he should be interested enough to pick up the phone and call. Texting should be reserved for occasions where either party cannot access a phone such as during a meeting or during class. Texting should not be used as a substitute for conversation, especially in a new relationship!

✓ **Set the standard!**

I don't have common relationship problems anymore because I set the standard. For those of you who don't know, common relationship problems are infidelity, staying out all night, not being sensitive to my needs, and disrespect! My girlfriends joke about me and say that I am the only woman they know who can break it off with someone one day and go out with someone new the next day.

Well, it's true. I don't throw pity parties or pick up the phone and cry to my girlfriends because a man has hurt me. I have no reason to cry when a relationship is over. Life is too short! I know that I will never in a lifetime be able to work my way through all of the men who genuinely "want" me. I will never be able to work my way through all those men who will be "good" to me. So why would I waste my time crying over someone who is not? I know my worth! I know what I have to offer to a man who is worthy of me. This is the attitude that *ALL* women need to adapt.

When a relationship is not working, it is easy for me to walk away because respect is not an option! It's a requirement. So many women make respect optional. It's as if they are saying to a man, "Ok, you don't have to respect me, and I am still going to be with you anyway!"

Learn to have a healthy relationship with yourself first and when you do, it will be easy to recognize your worth and what you can contribute to a potential relationship.

Part of understanding ourselves means understanding why we do the things we do. Why do women allow men to devalue us? Most of the time it comes down to the fact that he may be providing something that we can't provide for ourselves. As was discussed earlier, sometimes a woman suffering from low self-esteem may feel that she needs a man to complete her. It could be that he fills a financial need or a sexual need. Women become addicted to great sex. As you know, sometimes it can be difficult for a woman to find that man who provides really great, mind-blowing sex. So when we find that man that has the ability to make our toes curl and provide us with one Earth-shattering orgasm after another, we will cling to him as if our very existence depends on it. It is inconsequential that the rest of the relationship is not working. It doesn't matter that you are giving up too much of yourself, your time, money, or whatever your situation may be. We become emotionally attached to a man who knows how to put it down in the sex department. However, holding on to a man at any cost is not only unhealthy, it doesn't increase your worth in his eyes.

If you allow a man to continue to treat you badly, he will continue to do so. After all, you don't care so why should he?

Now that we have an idea of where we're going with this, let's move along so that we will know how to recognize a *good* man!

Recognizing a Good Man!

emember, before you can find a good man, you have to know what a good man is! If I had a nickel for each time I heard a woman say that there are no good men out there I'd be rich. Ladies, there is no shortage of good men. Even when you eliminate those that are married, gay, on drugs or in jail there is still an abundance of eligible, successful, attractive men out there. The problem isn't that they are not out there, but rather what qualities you might be looking for in a man. What are the personal qualities and characteristics that make a man a *good* man in your eyes?

Does having good credit make him a good man? Does taking care of his responsibilities make him a good man? Is it because he does things for you? Or maybe he is a good man because he is faithful and doesn't cheat? Maybe it's his attractiveness and his sexual abilities that make him a good man. Whatever the term "good man" means to you, you have to know exactly what qualities you're looking for. I can't tell you what qualities you should look for in a man. Only you can determine what your expectations and needs are from a potential mate. Every woman's needs are different, but I encourage you to understand what your expectations are before deciding to commit to a long-term relationship or marriage. Finding and getting that special man to put that ring on your finger in 365 days or less is not so much about him. It's about *YOU*!

Take an "eyes wide open" look at your relationship. Sometimes when things are going well in a relationship, it is easy for a woman to believe that she has a good man. We may not have experienced any hardships in life to test our man and the strength of our relationship. Hardships help a woman to open her eyes and evaluate the circumstances surrounding her relationship. For example, how would your man react if you were diagnosed with a debilitating illness or disease like cancer or diabetes? How would he react if you suddenly lost your job and couldn't work? Would he step in and assist you financially or take care of the kids? How would he react if a family member was ill and needed to move in with the both of you because they required constant care and supervision? These are all things you should consider when you are looking for a good man because life has a tendency to throw curve balls at you.

This is a situation that I came to terms with in a previous relationship. Four months after we began dating I got laid off from my job where I was earning in the mid-sixty-thousand dollar range working part-time. Before I was laid off, it was customary for me to take him out. I would treat him to lunches, dinners, shows, or whatever, just as he treated me. However, after the layoff, my financial situation took a drastic turn for the worse. Unemployment wasn't enough to cover my vehicle payment, let alone a $1,400 per month mortgage.

I had never been out of a job before, so this situation was totally new to me. I had always been so independent and I wasn't accustomed to asking for anything from my man.

During this period of unemployment I ultimately turned to all of my family members for financial assistance. They chipped in to help me out as best as they could, but I remember as I was discussing my finances with my seventy-two year old stepfather, I recall him saying that I needed a "Helpmate." I told him I had never heard that term used before, so he explained that I needed a man in my life that was going to take on a man's responsibility *if* he cared anything about me and wanted to be with me. I remember listening intently to my stepfather as he spoke about this, and I was overwhelmed with feelings of shame because I actually had a man that I was sleeping with *every* night who wasn't helping in *any* way.

At that point, I couldn't find work, I had depleted all of my resources and I realized that I didn't have much of a choice. I could either go to my man and ask for assistance or go without. Furthermore, I started to think about the fact that he and I were currently spending the majority of our time together; we spent every night together at either his home or mine. We spent so much time with each other it actually felt as if we were already living together, therefore, was it plausible to believe that I should be able to depend on him financially during this time of crisis in my life?

This was a difficult step for me to take because I had never been in this situation before. All of my life I'd had a job. I had always carried my own weight no matter who I was with. I had been in relationships with very well-known, prominent men and had never asked for their support. I have always been proud of the fact that I was Ms. Independent!

Shortly thereafter, I found myself having a very serious discussion with my man about my situation. Afterwards, he started doing the bare minimum so that he could continue to have a sexual relationship with me, like putting gas in my vehicle (although that was so I could run up and down the highway to see him), and buying a few groceries every now and then. However, I realized that he kept a running tally of what he spent on me. After ten months of being in this relationship, I realized that anything he inevitably helped me with was something that I had to specifically ask for; he never did anything just because he cared. In addition, he made me feel like I was a burden and any time he did anything for me, he never failed to bring up how much he had already spent on me.

In the meantime, all of my major bills were still unpaid. I was in jeopardy of losing my home and my vehicle, but to him it was nothing. He never showed any concern at all and still expected me to spend each and every night with him. From the outside looking in, everyone around me thought I was okay. They were all operating under the idea that even though I wasn't working I was still being taken care of because I had a good man. One who was working a civil service job and who was also career military. He had to be helping me out, right? This is what I mean, ladies. Looks can be deceiving.

We began having major arguments. Obviously he didn't like the fact that I expected him to assist me financially, even though he was the man that I'd been dating for the past year. We had discussed a future together, but he felt he was the last person I should come to for help. It was obvious to me that he didn't want to help me out, or as he stated, he didn't have it to help me with. However, if he didn't have it, there was reason for me to be confused as he bought expensive toys for himself all the time, like fifty-two inch flat screen televisions for each bedroom in his home, Blue Ray disc players, and expensive rifle collections. I even remember being with him once when he was considering buying a three hundred dollar spice rack! I began to resent him for being so selfish. He further displayed his selfishness by insisting that I go with him while he shopped for expensive items for *his* home. After a while, I refused to go shopping with him. It was crazy. I was so broke, sometimes I couldn't afford to buy food, but he wanted me to go with him while he purchased three hundred dollar spice racks! No thanks, I'll pass!

It was quite a journey, but this journey came to an end exactly one year to the date that I began dating him. I'd just gone back to work after having been laid off for eight months. I was working two jobs trying to recover from the time I spend unemployed. I would leave one job to go straight to another to work a twelve hour shift. I was stressed, losing weight, and couldn't sleep. I had a mountain of debt, my house was going into foreclosure and I was about to lose my car. Although we'd had this conversation before I went to him and simply said, "Please, help me! I'm not telling you what to do, but please help me figure out something!"

He got angry and his reply was "It's not my fault that you're in the shape that you're in."

Talk about a reality check!

It was quite a lesson about the choices that we can make regarding a man. As I said before, looks can be deceiving. It's easy to think you have a good man until a situation arises to test your relationship. I remember after the break-up receiving an e-mail from him where he stated that he felt our relationship was just bad timing, if I had not lost my job, everything would have been fine between us. But to me, our relationship had been perfect timing because had I never lost my job, I might have never known that I wouldn't be able to depend on him in my time of need. So sometimes it takes something to happen in order for you to see where you stand in a relationship. Anyone can be happy when times are good, but will he be there for you when times are bad?

There is another funny twist to this story. After I ended the relationship, my ex discovered that someone else was interested in me, and in hopes of deterring the interest of this other man he emailed him a copy of all of my bills! The email included the monthly amounts that I owed on my car, my mortgage payment, loan payments (to include interest rates) and even my utility bills. I was floored! I would never have imagined that someone that I had been so close to would actually stoop so low. Ironically, the gentleman who was on the receiving end of this email never responded back to my bitter ex, but instead, he sent an email to me and CC'ed a copy to my ex. In his email he stated that although someone found it necessary to inform him of my financial obligations he wasn't interested in my credit report, he was interested in me and a *real* man would not tear a woman down, but try to help her up. Not only is this man now one of my dearest friends, but he is also one of the true *good* men out there. Even when he knew of my financial struggles, he still wanted to be there.

I felt it necessary to share this lesson with you, ladies, because it could possibly help you take a closer look at *your* relationship. Before going through the ordeal of losing my job, I was one of those women who bragged to my girlfriends about how great my man was. Fact was, I didn't even know myself!

Another thing I've found is that sometimes a woman will want a man so badly, but she may not even know *why* she wants him. I have found that some women care more about being part of a couple than they do about having a mentally and emotionally healthy relationship. A woman who takes the time to develop a healthy state of mind will usually have a healthy relationship. So, even though your mission may be to get your man, take the focus off of him and put it on you. Once you make *YOU* the priority, he doesn't have a choice but to fall in line *if* he wants you, because you're making it understood that you won't accept anything less. It makes a huge difference when you realize *why* you're doing something. Don't do it because your girlfriends told you to and don't do it just because everyone else is doing it.

There are some young ladies out there just following a trend of what society depicts as right. For example, a few weeks ago while interviewing some young women for the radio show that week; I asked them, "How soon is too soon to have sex with someone that you just met?" I wanted to know how they felt about the topic and which rule they lived by. I got a lot of interesting feedback. One response in particular was from a twenty-three year old who told me that she had a three month rule. On the surface that sounded great until I asked her why. She replied, "Because Joan on the television show *Girlfriends* has a three month rule. And if it's good enough for Joan it's good enough for me." I thought this was so funny, but this is the reality of how some young women think. They don't know why they do some of the things that they do, they're just following a trend!

My point is: there is nothing wrong with having rules as long as you understand why you have that rule. Don't just do something because someone else is doing it! This is why my writing and my radio show are so important to me. There are many young women out there who need some direction and if they can read my books, listen to my show, and take something away that they can use, then it makes all of my hard work worthwhile. I may not have all the answers and if I don't, I can definitely try to point them in the right direction. Young ladies just don't have many adult role models these days. So, to my sisters out there who have it together, it is our responsibility to step in and mentor some of these young girls.

Can you recognize a dead-end relationship? The fact is, most women can't identify when they are in a dead-end relationship. For those of you who don't know, a dead-end relationship is classified as one that is not progressively moving forward; a relationship in which one person's needs are not being met.

Everyone doesn't have the same needs in a relationship, which is why it is best to choose a partner whose needs are compatible with yours. In order for a relationship to work you must share some of the same principles and values, as well as share a similar lifestyle. Generally, the more you have in common with your partner the better you will get along. The more we have in common with someone, the more comfortable and trusting we feel towards that person. Relationships are difficult enough as it is, but sometimes when you're not compatible, simple problems become major issues.

For example, if you don't smoke, it may be wise not to marry a smoker. This is a simple issue, but it is one that actually came up in one of my previous marriages. I don't smoke, however, my ex-husband did. We initially began our relationship by being respectful to one another. Knowing that I was a non-smoker, he agreed to smoke his cigars outside our home. However, as the marriage progressed and he started to get comfortable, I would return home to smell the toxic fumes of smoke lingering in the air. Although I knew he had been smoking in our home, he would always deny it. This might seem a small thing to some, but it contributed to bigger issues and it was a clear lack of respect for my wishes. This is why it is important to have similar lifestyles.

Having similar lifestyles does not mean that you have to be exact in every way. Some people are perfectly matched and they are exact opposites. For example, my man and I are in some ways exact opposites. He is extremely laid back and often teases me by saying that I am easily excited. However, we share the same vision, drive, determination, and entrepreneurial spirit. We share the same beliefs and common goals. We have a similar communication style and it makes our relationship so much easier. It can be difficult to maintain a relationship when both parties have totally different lifestyles.

What if the relationship isn't working? I do not encourage anyone to remain in a relationship that is not working on all levels. When you do, someone usually ends up hurt. You would be surprised at how many times I have asked women who were in dead-end relationships, "If it's not working, why is it so difficult to let go?" And I hear, "I don't know!"

Ladies, if you don't know why you love your man, or why you want to be his wife, he may not be the one! And if you don't know, clearly you don't know you, so I suggest you take some much needed time away from a man and the confusion of a relationship and get to know you!

Women want everything, but over the years I have learned that realistically we can't have everything. Furthermore, I'm not sure if there is any man in existence that makes up every-

thing that women want. The only perfect men are in fairy
tales, and I'm not so sure that many of them are perfect either.

Comedian Katt Williams did an excellent job of depicting
how women are about men. In his act, he says that women set
our sights too high. He is quick to say how women can have a
98% good man — one who goes to work every day, earns a
paycheck, brings that check home, puts gas in our rides and
even takes better care of our children than he takes of his
own — yet, because we (women) are greedy, we will throw
back the 98% man because he is lacking 2%.

To hear Katt Williams say this is funny, but it's true.
Women are always searching for that 100% man. But realistically, can we really expect to find that 100% man if we're not
100% ourselves?

When you set expectations of what you want from your
relationship, make sure you set some goals to get yourself
together first. You will always find yourself in a better
position when you may *want*, but don't actually *need* a man.
Ask yourself a few essential questions. Are you able to stand
on your own and provide for yourself without any assistance?
Do you know your FICO credit score and are you comfortable
with it? These are all essential elements that will make you a
value to the man in your life. A man wants a woman who is
also going to bring something to the table. Not someone he
constantly has to rescue. So make sure you are at least what
you're expecting from your man. If you expect him to be
financially secure, you should be financially secure. If you
expect his credit to be better than average, then so should
yours.

Now we understand that everyone is capable of having
some downfalls. With the economy as it is today people are

losing jobs at an alarming rate. Just look at my own personal situation that I shared with you earlier. Things happen and we have to be able to adapt to changes in life. If you are one of those women who are experiencing some financial struggles, we are going to discuss how you can get your finances back on track. Don't give up because everything is fixable. If I can come out of a financial crunch, so can you. In the section entitled *Developing Your Financial Self* I will give you the tools that you need to get back on the right track.

Most women seem to have one common need when it comes to what we want from our relationships—stability and security. We want a man who is a protector and provider, one who is honest and trustworthy, one who is loyal and faithful, one who loves us unconditionally, as well as one who supports and celebrates our accomplishments. None of these wants are unrealistic. These are qualities that you should expect from your man.

Realistically, men are not that much different in their wants. A real man wants to be a protector and provider and he needs that emotional support from the woman that he loves. A man needs to feel that as his woman, *you* are his biggest supporter, his biggest fan and his biggest cheerleader. So, never fail to let your man know how much you love, respect, and admire him.

Another aspect of a relationship is weeding out the men who seek to play games. The world is full of game players, manipulators and opportunists. It would be unrealistic to think that they don't exist. Some women assume that most men are only out to find a good time, and in some cases it's true. Some men get a thrill out of running game on multiple women. And if you are like me, I'm sure you have come across

a few players in your day. In my twenties it was bad. However, as I got older, I began to realize I couldn't place blame on
men for being manipulative. I had to blame myself for not
using my head or my God-given ability to make educated
decisions. When a man told me something that didn't make
sense or add up, I made excuses and rationalized it to fit what
I wanted.

Today I have a zero tolerance policy when it comes to
nonsense. Oftentimes, when you initially meet a man, whether
it's in a club, bar, or on the street, he doesn't see beyond that
moment. He doesn't think: *Could she be the one I want to spend
the rest of my life with?* The only thing he knows at that particular moment is that he finds you attractive, and yes, he is
hoping for a good time.

His way of thinking makes most women classify him as a
dog or a player, but whether or not he will be a dog or a player
depends on you. Let's take a look and examine the basic rule
of being a player. It takes no talent or skill to be a player.
Everyone has the ability to play someone, even you. So, when
you come across a man who initially shows you signs of only
being interested in you for sex, money, gifts or whatever else
you can offer him, don't waste your time and move on
because there are other men out there who are looking for
exactly what you are looking for, a healthy loving relationship!
When a man sees that he cannot run game on you he will
usually *run* in the opposite direction. He sees that you won't
tolerate it and he would much rather look for an easier target.
So if he runs, let him run. You don't want to put up with that
nonsense anyway!

Now let's take note of where we are. We know that we are
mentally and emotionally ready for a relationship; we have
established our expectations and determined how to recognize
a good man, now let's master the basics!

Start With the Basics *Love Thy Self*

$\mathcal{I}$t's a known fact that men are visual creatures by nature, so this is where we will begin. I start with the physical attributes of a woman because we all know that men are drawn initially to physically attractive women. We have already established the fact that being physically attractive doesn't necessarily mean that you have to be 120 pounds, or even be *pretty* by the rigid standards of society. But it appears that society is changing its standards. There was a time when it was fashionable to be damn near anorexic, now we see the acceptance of a variety of body shapes, sizes, and ethnicities. Attractive does not necessarily mean good-looking, it just means that a woman has to have a certain appeal about herself that the other person likes. Most men define an attractive woman as one who takes care of herself, meaning one who is concerned about her appearance and her overall health. Your actual size doesn't matter; the important thing is that you must feel comfortable in your own skin.

Men are not as conscious about the physical aspects of the body as most women think. Yes, men do love nice bodies and pretty faces, but they define "pretty" as sexy. Think about it, how many times have you known a man to cheat, then you see that the woman he is cheating with doesn't look as attractive as his woman? Men love desirable women, and the women that they choose appeals to their sexual side. So you should always make yourself physically appealing to your man.

This is important because how physically attractive a man finds you determines how much time he will want to spend with you. Always remember, before a man can care about *who* a woman is, he must first get past *how* a woman looks.

I have a motto that I live by, and it is: **"Think sexy, be sexy!"** When women learn and live by this one rule, they have already won half the battle. Men desire women who are sexy. Sexy is a state of mind and a woman doesn't have to be a size 4 to be sexy. Sexy is not about your body. Sexy is about confidence. How one feels about herself is sexy. However, the better the condition your body is in, the more confident you will be. Even when it seems like men are not overly concerned with your looks, never let your guard down. This also includes when you are in the privacy of your own home.

Women are creatures of habit and unfortunately during our lives, many of us have picked up some bad habits. When we are in the privacy of our own home, it's easy to become comfortable and forget all those little extra things that we did in the beginning in order to get our man. We forget the effort we took in order to make sure that he saw us looking our best at all times. You know what I'm talking about, every time he came around your hair was combed, you smelled good and don't forget how you used to shimmy around in something sexy!

For some of you those days are long gone. You have traded in that perfectly coiffed hair for rollers and that awful, disgusting rag that some of you wear on your heads. That sexy lingerie has been traded in for Scooby-Doo pajamas. Let's face it, ladies, you got comfortable and now you are in a rut. Breaking those bad habits can be quite a challenge, but the good thing about habits is that it's just as easy to form new ones. By using the principles in this book you will develop new habits that will gain positive results, whether you are looking for a new relationship or to revive an old one.

Most women don't realize that she actually holds the most power in a relationship and she doesn't have to be a super-model to capture a man's mind and imagination. We have the ability to *make* a man fall in love with us. You, as a woman, possess the natural ability to influence a man to your way of thinking and make him want to spend the rest of his life with you. But first, you must understand your power and know how to use that power to your benefit in order to gain the man of your dreams.

Never underestimate the power of persuasion! Women naturally possess this. It has been that way since the beginning of time. Look at Adam and Eve. Eve had the power to persuade Adam to do something he was already warned *not* to do. And it hasn't changed. Women still possess the power of persuasion over men. If you know how to use your body language and communicate correctly, you can make men feel the same kind of powerful sexual attraction to you that you feel. And it's relatively easy!

This is not a game, nor is it manipulation. There is absolutely nothing wrong in training yourself in what it takes to get your man. If you want to participate in the Olympics you would train. Preparing yourself for a career in law or the medical field requires years of extensive schooling and train-ing so that you are well educated in those fields. So, you should look at getting your man the same way. Educate yourself on what it takes, identify what a man wants and needs from his relationship, and you can be those things by simply being yourself. When you learn the secret of loving yourself, you will effortlessly become this attractive person that men won't be able to resist. And what's more is that you won't have to mold yourself into someone you're not.

Overall sexiness is about attitude, and your attitude determines how people perceive you. We've all seen the makeover shows where these ordinary women for various different reasons are not happy with themselves or their physical appearance and decide that they need a makeover. They suffer from low self-esteem and a lack of self-confidence and ask to be transformed. We see the ordinary woman before the transformation, and she is just that, quite ordinary, but after the makeover she is beautiful, sexy, and confident. She has attitude.

I wasn't always the self-assured woman that I am today. As a matter of fact, it took a long time for me to view myself as sexy, especially when I was growing up. As a young woman, I was skinny, flat-chested, with big lips and kinky hair. I was also extremely self-conscious and withdrawn. I wouldn't talk to or make eye contact with anyone if I could avoid it. But over the years, I learned to transform my attitude by working on myself. I learned that I had the power to change the things about myself that I wasn't happy with. When I made these internal changes I became more confident on the exterior. As a result, my self-esteem soared. I was still skinny and flat-chested, but I learned that I had assets; full lips and nicely shaped legs, which men loved.

All women have assets. As a woman, you have to discover what your assets are and learn how to display them to benefit you, which we will talk about in more detail in a later section. While building my self-esteem, I learned to make eye contact with strangers, I began to flirt, and I began to voice my opinions, views, and ideas. Not only to men, but to everyone I came in contact with. I learned to be heard, seen and respected. And the biggest lesson that I've learned is: *If there is something that you don't like about yourself, change it!*

Through all of my research, I learned what men really wanted, what they found attractive and I became that. Not for a man, but for me. I wanted to boost my own self-esteem and when I developed this attitude, I found that I like who I am. I didn't change who I was, I just had to *discover* who I was. Still today, I may not have the best body in the world, but what I do have is confidence. And confidence is sexy! I am so confident now that I can walk into a room full of gorgeous people and I am guaranteed to turn the heads of men *and* women. Why you ask? It's because my attitude projects an air of confidence which is so naturally attractive. A naturally attractive woman who possesses confidence will be able to walk into a room and command it. She won't have to get loud or even speak a word, but her presence alone will speak volumes. It will draw people to you.

So how do you develop confidence?

The first thing I want you to do is take a look in the mirror and take note of what you see. Take note of your strengths and weaknesses. Critique yourself and decide what you don't like. Do a self-analysis from head to toe.

We know that men like different things in different women. Some like short hair while others like it long. Some like thin women while others like them thick. We won't get so caught up in the specifics here; all we want to do is make sure that we present our best face to the world. Generally, women that take care of themselves are more attractive than those that do not. Let's agree that in order to attract the best you must look your best! There are some things that are necessary in order to achieve and attain your goal of capturing a man's attention. Look at the condition of your skin, teeth, hands and feet. In a nutshell, these are the things that a man notices first.

Let's break each item down starting with the things you can control:

✓ **Skin**

Men do *not* find facial hair on a woman attractive. If you have more facial hair than he does, this could be a problem and could possibly keep you from finding your Mr. Right.

Men love women with smooth, blemish-free faces. If you have a problem with severe acne, you may consider making a trip to the dermatologist.

Please do not use makeup as a cover-up for bad skin. Most of the time, it only makes the problem worse. If your case is severe enough, do yourself a favor and consult a professional.

✓ **Teeth - take note of your smile.**

Most people tend to overlook the condition of their mouth. I don't understand this because it's also the first thing that people see. Look in the mirror; are your teeth cracked, crooked or dingy? Are your gums swollen, do they bleed when you brush? If so, these are obvious signs of dental problems and you should see a dental care provider immediately. If you do not have any obvious dental problems, your mouth should be in good condition and your breath should smell clean and fresh.

How do you know if your breath smells? Okay, I know this sounds crazy, but believe it or not, some people have lived with bad breath for so long they can't tell that it smells.

I remember dating a guy who had a problem with bad breath. He was good-looking, intelligent, successful, and he had bad breath. Initially, I tried offering him breath mints, but over time, as I started getting to know him better, I noticed that he was doing all the right things; brushing, flossing, and rinsing, but his mouth still smelled. Finally, I had to tell him that maybe he should consider seeing a dentist because of his mouth odor. It was embarrassing, but he agreed to get checked out. When he did, he found out that he had gingivitis, a periodontal disease. Routine dental visits should be something that you never skip.

✓ Hands and feet

I'm not going to get too deep into this, but these are body parts that are displayed when someone meets you. Look at it this way, your hands should always be ready for your Mr. Right to place that ring on your finger. Your nails should always be neat and clean. Nothing is less attractive than a woman with chipped nail polish on her hands or toe nails. Nothing is less sexy than calloused and rough heels. So spend a little time getting the basics together. Once you know what to do and how to do it, you too can get the man you want to put a ring on your finger in 365 days or less. Men would also be wise to take this advice. I have come across too many men in my day whose feet look like they have been walking over hot coals. So, guys, keep in mind, an occasional pedicure doesn't make you feminine; it shows that you care about your personal hygiene and grooming.

It is important to remember that: *Even when it seems like men are not overly concerned with your looks, never let your guard down.* Keep yourself together at all times.

✓ Get your swagger on!

Every woman needs something that's all her own—her signature walk! This is the one thing that is guaranteed to capture a man's attention and it is the one thing that he will remember most. A woman's walk displays her level of confidence. A man can determine your level of confidence simply by observing the way you walk. Women have swagger, too, so let it show!

✓ *"Think sexy, be sexy!"* Remember my motto.

Always make a habit of wearing sexy underwear! Matching bras and panties are a must. Some women are religious about keeping their favorite old, worn-out underwear because they claim that it is comfortable. But I can assure you that men do not find faded fabric and dry-rotted elastic sexy, so get rid of it. You don't want your man seeing those, not even by accident. Sexy underwear is not only for your man, but it's for you too. When you wear it, it can actually make you feel sexy.

Awhile back, one of my best girlfriend's and I were going out. When I arrived at her house to pick her up, she wasn't dressed, so I sat on her bed and we talked as she was trying to decide what she wanted to wear. As we were talking, with no prior warning, she dropped her robe to the floor and I screamed, "Augh! What do you have on?" She had on a faded black bra, and some beige colored, stretched-out cotton granny panties, that looked like they used to be white.

She looked down at herself and asked, "What?"

I replied, "No wonder your man won't have sex with you!"

She said, "Girl, I work a full-time job, then I come home and take care of these children. I don't have time to worry about what I put on. If he ain't happy, he can go elsewhere!"

Well, eventually, he did!

Women spend too much time worrying about how the outside world sees us and not enough time worrying about how our man sees us. When we go out, we take extra time making sure our makeup is together and that every hair is in place. We make sure we have the perfect outfit with the perfect pair of shoes. But what's funny is when we are at home with our man we will sit around in faded sweats or Sponge Bob pajamas.

The point is, whether married or single, all it takes to keep the excitement alive in a relationship is a little creativity. You've got to know what your man wants. If it's sex, make sure you give him something that will have him at work watching the clock counting down the minutes until he can get home to you.

Get out of those shorts and tee-shirts. During a poll I asked married men—and men who were in long-term committed relationships—what their woman wore to bed. The highest percentage said, (and not very happily) shorts and tee-shirts.

Ladies, although *you* might find shorts and tee-shirts comfortable, I can assure you that your man is less than impressed with your comfortable nightwear. We already know that men live for fantasy. They watch porn and go to strip clubs for that fantasy, so incorporate a little bit of fantasy into your everyday life. When you provide that fantasy, your man will enjoy coming home to you.

Every woman should own a collection of sexy underwear. It doesn't have to be anything extreme, and since there are so many styles to choose from, it makes it easy to find garments that are flattering, yet comfortable. Remember, men love being in the presence of sensual women. This is just one of many things women can do to ensure that she appeals to that special man in her life. All of the tips covered in this book are going to contribute to the magnificent creature you are that no man will be able to resist. But in order for the principles to work, you have to want it. In my experience, I have found that many women complain about what they want and what they are not getting from their relationship, but they don't want to invest the time and effort to achieve it. It's like losing weight, everyone wants to do it, but not many are willing to put forth the effort it takes to lose those unwanted pounds.

I am just as guilty when it comes to this issue. Right now I could stand to lose about fifteen pounds, and if I put forth the effort I could do it quite easily. However, when it comes time for me to eliminate all the goodies from my fridge, I realize that I'm not quite ready to give up the donuts, cakes and pies, or my occasional cocktails. So, I always find myself making excuses as to why I'll commit to it later. The same principles apply when trying to get your man to place that ring on your finger. You have to make the necessary changes in order to attain your goal, if you really want it. Just like anything else worth having, it takes commitment and sacrifice. Then again, not every woman wants to get married.

My girlfriend Cassandra is an independent woman in every sense of the word. She has a career that she loves; she is in her mid-thirties and has no children. She has also been in a long-term, committed relationship with her man for several years. They live together and she loves him, but she has absolutely no desire to get married. She claims she is satisfied with her situation exactly as it is. This holds true for other women as well. Not every woman wants to get married and there is absolutely nothing wrong with that. But for those who do, you need to have a plan, and you must be willing to put in the necessary work so that you are marriage material.

Just the other day a young lady, who I recently met online, said to me, "Why should I have to *make* my relationship work? I don't want to *make* it work, it should just work!"

Unfortunately, relationships like anything else just don't work that way. Time, energy, and effort, is required to nurture a relationship. The key to getting your man to want to make you his wife is quite simple. You must be the woman he wants to marry. He needs to feel that by getting married to you his life will be improved. Most men marry when he feels in some way it will benefit him. How you benefit him depends on what he's looking for, this is why you must know what your man wants. So, it is in your best interest to ensure that your man recognizes your value.

When a man is in love with you, he will marry simply because he feels that by losing you he'll be missing out on something. He also won't be able to tolerate the thought of someone else being with the woman he loves. Men usually become engaged quickly when they realize: *Hey, I have something good here...I can't lose her!* Sometimes, even if he never thought about marriage before, the way he perceives you can give him that little push he may need to help him make up his mind.

Women always say that good men are hard to find, but men say it is even harder to find a good woman. When men refer to a "good" woman, he means one that encompasses everything he is looking for. So when he happens to find it, you better believe he won't take a chance on losing it. So what are his options? He'll marry her!

A man will know quickly whether the woman he is involved with is marriage material. It won't take him years to make up his mind. This also depends on the stage of the relationship that you are in. Are you casually dating, or are you in a serious committed relationship where you are spending nights at each other's homes? Do you spend the majority of the day (outside of work) together? Have you discussed a future together?

The more advanced the relationship, the easier it will be to determine if there is any possibility of marriage. Based on my personal experiences—and the interviews I have conducted with men—normally it only takes about six to nine months for a man to really know if he wants a woman to be his wife. Ladies, you will be able to tell if he considers you wife material if you take note of the signs. The signs are always there.

So, if you have been involved with a man for years and he's still telling you he doesn't know if he's ready, trust me... he's not going to marry you. He's just biding his time, waiting to see if something better is going to come along. If by some chance he does finally decide to marry you after years of being in a relationship with you, he probably finally realized that his chances of finding someone better are slim to none. In any case, if you are in a situation where your man has been stringing you along for an extended amount of time, you may as well move along, so that you will be available when you do meet that potential Mr. Right.

Developing Your 'Sexual' Self

$\mathcal{I}$f there is one thing I'm sure of, it's that every woman has a sexual diva inside just waiting to be released. I'm sure many of you will agree that self-esteem issues are a big hindrance for most women, especially when it comes to intimacy with our partner. Not only do we deal with the emotional issues associated with changes to our bodies due to aging, childbirth, and surgeries due to health problems; we also allow those insecurities to affect intimacy with our partner. We worry about what our partner sees when he looks at us.

I frequently hear from women who say they hate to undress in front of their man because they have stretch marks, sagging breasts and have put on a few extra pounds. Nobody faults you for having these emotions because it is natural to suffer from insecurities. At some point we all do. There are so many factors about life that we can't change and the fact that we get older is one of them. However, although you can't change the fact that you are getting older, you can change your mindset about the process.

As I'm writing this book, I am approaching my forty-fourth birthday and I welcome it. I have grown in so many aspects of my life. I look at the previous forty plus years as a journey that I had to go through to get to where I am today. I will be the first to admit that I don't have the best body in the world. Ironically, I am more confident and secure about my body now, than when I was in my twenties. When I weighed 125 pounds I was very insecure and self-conscious about my body. I wasn't happy with my appearance. My butt wasn't big enough, my boobs were too small. Now at age forty-four, my body has gone through some changes; drastic changes due to surgical scars, weight gain and loss, and life in general, but guess what? I am a sexy somebody! I am an ordinary lady, with an extraordinary attitude! So in this chapter, we're going to learn how to be FABULOUS in the skin that we're in!

This section is about self-discovery. It is designed to teach you to be comfortable in your own skin. In order to become a sexually desirable woman you must first discover who you are. I am in tune with my sexuality because I know who I am. Another reason I think I'm so in tune with my body is because I was my own first lover. I learned the art of pleasing myself at the age of thirteen. Without my parents' knowledge, I began using my allowance and purchasing *Cosmopolitan* magazines when I was eleven years old. I was an avid reader at that age. What stood out the most in all of the books and magazines I read, were the stories and articles about the "Big O."

Even at that young age, I wanted to know what they were talking about. I began experimenting and tried on many occasions to create this feeling that I had read about that would result in an orgasm. To my disappointment, I couldn't seem to get it right. I became increasing frustrated because I was a smart girl and by following the instructions I should have been able to create this orgasmic feeling that I had read so much about.

My problem was I didn't know the difference in the actual body parts. So when the instructions said to stimulate the clitoris, I didn't know the clitoris from the vagina. I thought, *It's not that big of an area, so how hard can it possibly be to find it?* Boy was I simple! But I was only thirteen, so it was understandable.

At the time, my stepfather would leave his *Playboy* magazine's laying around the house. I remember after so many failed attempts at trying my make myself have an orgasm, I got one of his magazines that spelled out the 'how to' instructions in detail. I went into the bathroom and got comfortable on the floor. It took me twenty minutes, but, baby, I got there! *Whew!* It was one of the greatest learning experiences of my life. I've always felt that being able to pleasure myself was one of the contributing factors as to how I was able to remain a virgin until I was nineteen years old.

The point is, today I know myself so well that I can pleasure myself in two minutes flat. So again, I say that the best way to discover who you are is to learn yourself. You can't expect a man to pleasure you if you can't pleasure yourself.

I am still amazed today at the number of women who admit that they have never had an orgasm. Not even during intercourse! Ladies, I'm here to tell you that it is much easier to get your man to please you when you know what it takes. Achieving an orgasm during intercourse can be somewhat tricky if you don't know what area(s) of your body responds to stimulation. All it takes to learn what does it for you is to do a little self-discovery and learn your body. You should be so familiar with your body that even in the dark you know how the person you're with sees you. Therefore, I suggest getting up close and personal with yourself.

We touched on doing a basic self-analysis in the previous section, but now we are going to take it a step further and really concentrate on our sexual self. Stand nude in front of a full length mirror. The objective is to familiarize yourself with your body. Study your appearance from every angle. Don't be ashamed of the woman you see staring back at you. Embrace her, love her, and if you don't already know her, get to know her. Take note honestly of your assets as well as your weaknesses.

All women have assets and you have to discover what your assets are. You have to assess yourself in order to know what you're working with. Lingerie can be your best friend *if* you know how to select it! Let me tell you why I speak so incessantly about lingerie. One of my best friends owns a kiosk in the mall that happens to be parked right in front of Victoria's Secret. One day, I happened to be hanging out with her as she worked. I began watching the males' faces as they passed the lingerie display window. No matter their previous demeanor, as they passed the display window, they all perked up. Just looking at the scantily clad mannequins was enough to give each man who passed something to think about. So ladies, don't downplay the importance of sexy lingerie.

The greatest thing about lingerie is, no matter your body type, there is a style designed to compliment you. Being sexy is about enhancing your assets. Don't worry so much about your weaknesses; with a little creativity, it is easy to disguise your flaws. For example, if your best features are your breasts and your worst is your stomach; select outfits that will enhance your breasts to your advantage. Consider a garment designed to divert attention away from your stomach such as a corset or bustier that is designed to slim the waistline and accentuate the bust-line.

Always enhance your best assets. My best assets are my legs, so of course, no matter what outfit I'm wearing you will always see me in a pair of killer stilettos!

Now that you have identified your assets you are ready to get your gear. Remember, selecting sexy lingerie can be a time consuming endeavor. Don't think you will be able to walk into Victoria's Secret, grab a few items and expect the look you are trying to achieve to automatically fall into place. So take your time when selecting your sexy attire. And since undergarments are usually non-returnable, be sure to try on your selections before making your purchases and leaving the store.

Also, be careful of shopping online for the same reason. In many cases, if your purchases don't fit they may not be returnable. So I suggest buying when you have adequate time to try the items on. You want your sexy garments to look good on you, but you also want to feel comfortable in them, so experiment with different styles and colors.

If you're not accustomed to wearing sexy underwear it may be necessary to get used to wearing it and gaining confidence in it before you make your big reveal in front of your man. In this case, it is a good idea to get used to it when you are at home alone. Set up your mirrors; practice different poses to see how you look best. Study your reflection and look at yourself from your man's perspective. Don't forget your heels! High heel shoes are the greatest invention ever created. No matter your body type or what outfit you are wearing, heels make you look sexy and they accentuate your legs. Not to mention men love them! On a personal note, if you are not used to wearing heels start out small. Don't just jump into a pair of six inch stilettos if you can't walk in them. Your goal is to look sexy, not silly. Advance slowly from a two inch heel and progress upward.

If your new look is something that is totally out of the ordinary for you it can feel awkward the first time out. This is why it is important to get used to the feel of your new attire at home alone before you decide to reveal it to your man for the first time.

Once you are finally ready for your big reveal, try placing a few candles around the room to soften the lighting and create a more romantic atmosphere. Act casual, walk around in your new underwear like it is the most natural thing ever. This is guaranteed to get your man's attention. Remember sexuality is about attitude. You are totally in control. It's knowing that you are sexy that gives you power. So work it, girl!

Developing Your 'Financial' Self!

*O*kay, ladies, I know most of you are probably wondering why you need financial counseling in order to get your man to put that ring on your finger in 365 days or less.

Well, ladies, it's like this, a man wants a woman who is bringing *something* to the table. You have to increase your value to your man in order to make him want you as his wife. It is simply not enough to be beautiful, captivating, and a twenty-four hour sexual goddess. When it comes to building a lifetime, a man is looking for more. He desires a woman with whom he can build a partnership. Even though he may be capable of taking care of everything, he needs to know that his woman is capable of being financially responsible and accountable.

There are many reasons why it is important to establish some financial independence. As the lyrics to Ne-Yo's and Jamie Foxx's hit song go, "I love her 'cause she got her own." A man does indeed love a woman who has her own. No matter how successful and wealthy a man may be, he needs to know that as his woman, you will protect those assets. He needs to know that he can trust you with his assets. Men don't hang around for the long haul with a woman he constantly has to rescue. Women who are able to be an asset, and not a liability, are those women that men find absolutely irresistible.

Many years ago, I was in a relationship with a well-known NFL player. He always said that of all the people around him, male and female, I was the only one who never asked for anything. I was the only one who would pick up the tab for dinner, drinks and entertainment. For him, this was unusual. He was accustomed to being with females who always wanted something, but never gave anything. And it was true, I was dating a man who was worth millions and I never asked him for anything. I always had my own money and I never needed anything that I couldn't provide on my own. My independence was one of the things that he found attractive about me.

All my life I considered myself to be that *independent* woman. Growing up, my father taught me to be self-sufficient, so I have always held down a job and I knew the importance of having my own money.

As I grew older, there have been times over the years I made some very sound business decisions, but I also recognize that I went through some periods of financial irresponsibility.

Like most women, I love nice things, and when I wanted something I planned to get it at whatever cost. It didn't matter if I couldn't afford it, I would find a way to afford it. It didn't matter if it would end up costing me thousands of dollars in interest, I would deal with that when the time came. Sometimes, I would not pay a credit card bill because I had found a pair of shoes that I absolutely had to have right then. So that credit card payment could wait. As a result, I would have to pay an additional thirty to forty dollars in late payment fees. I would overdraw an account to purchase something that I wanted immediately when payday was only a few days away.

That same item ended up costing me an extra thirty five dollars in overdraft fees. This is what I mean by financial irresponsibility, and at many times in my life, I lived this way.

Earlier, I shared a situation that I found myself in when I was laid off from a previous job. I never expected to lose my job, so I wasn't prepared when it happened. This experience forced me to take a look at my financial history. Although I was making good money prior to being laid off, I lived above my means. Sometimes I bought things I didn't need just because I had the money. My stepfather would always say to me, "You need to save something for a rainy day." My reply would always be the same, "But it's raining today!"

Losing my job made me look back and think how I could have been better prepared for that period of unemployment if I had made better decisions with my finances.

Although you may be financially responsible, sometimes life happens and we find ourselves in financial crunches that we can't do anything about. In my past, I have also experienced some of those challenges. When I developed breast cancer, my surgeries, chemotherapy treatments, radiation therapy, and finally, my reconstructive surgeries provided me with medical bills totaling close to two hundred thousand dollars. I knew that I could never in a lifetime pay that off, so you know what I did? Nothing! I did absolutely nothing!

However, when I was ready to buy a house and the car that I wanted, my credit was less than perfect, well... a whole *lot* less than perfect. But I figured, I had money, so who cares about my credit score? Instead, I paid a much higher price through the increased interest rates.

Finally, one day after struggling to pay off a mountain of debt, I woke up and realized I couldn't do it anymore. I was exhausted, and I felt as if I was borrowing from Peter to pay Paul! I had to have a fresh start, and for me, debt consolidation was the answer. Since then I have learned that with a new start you can live comfortably off any amount of money *if* you make responsible financial decisions. It took me some time (and an excellent credit repair firm) to raise my FICO score to a level that I'm comfortable with, and every day I'm working to get it higher.

Ok, ladies, I am not sharing these embarrassing personal experiences with you because I'm proud of it. I am sharing it because I hope that someone out there can learn and benefit from all of the mistakes that I've made. I hope that by sharing it might prevent you from making some of those same mistakes. If you don't take anything else away from this book, please take this, your financial future is your life! Don't do it for a man, do it for you! The following are a set of rules that can help you get your finances back on track.

• Set a budget and stick with it. This sounds much simpler than what it really is. Setting a budget and sticking to it is like losing weight. You have to have a plan. Remember what I said earlier about making something a ritual until it becomes a habit? This is how you have to look at this.

• Pay all bills on time, and if you can afford it, always pay more than the minimum due.

• Never ever, ever, ever, use your overdraft just because it's there! Don't do it! It's a trick; this is how banks get you!

• Allow yourself "occasional" small luxuries.

• No matter where you work or how much you earn, always stack some money away into a savings account, CD, IRA or some type of retirement plan. I know in this tough economy and with the problems many have experienced with investments, it can make you leery of where you are putting your money. However, you should always make having some type of savings fund a priority. Consult with a licensed financial planner to learn more about the best options for you.

• When purchasing large items such as vehicles never accept high interest rates. If a salesman tells you that due to a poor credit rating, your interest rate is in the 10% - 30% range. Just walk away! Get your finances together first, then go buy that car.

• Do not accept credit cards or loans just because a bank or financial institution offers it to you. Just say no!

• Have an emergency fund where if needed you can access funds immediately.

• Keep one credit card on hand for emergency purposes only.

• Use debit cards versus credit cards. I love the freedom of debit cards because I can't spend what I don't have. In addition to that, I feel much safer giving a creditor a debit card number versus a credit card. Debit cards allow you more control over your spending.

- Stop creating new debt and start paying off current debt. After paying off current debt, don't create unnecessary new debt.

- The absolute worst thing you can do is to do nothing! If you see that you are too far under and that you will never see daylight as it relates to your bills, it is never too late to get a fresh start. Consult an attorney or a credit or financial professional to find out what your options are. Oh yeah, please don't be like one of the many people I know who have filed bankruptcy to get out of debt and end up in worse shape two years later.

Okay, ladies, now you are mentally ready, you know your sexual self, you've got your financial self together (or you're working on a plan), now it's time to go get that ring!

Be Approachable!

adies, no matter where you meet your man I cannot say enough, let your body language show that you are open and approachable.

Years ago, one of my girlfriends used to practice what I call a very direct and unrealistic approach. This approach almost never works, and on the rare occasion that it does work, you could find yourself in a situation where you could be exchanging sex for money. I remember an incident where I was out with a girlfriend, and I happened to walk up to her as an extremely attractive man approached her. As I walked up, I could hear her saying with an attitude, *"If you're not trying to take care of me and my three kid's you may as well keep moving!"*

Her words were filled with such attitude and hostility. Of course, the man, without ever saying a word, walked away. I looked at my girlfriend in amazement and said, "No wonder you can't find a man! Can a man at least get your name *before* he starts paying your bills and taking care of your kids?" She replied that she didn't want to waste anyone's time, nor did she want anyone wasting hers.

This is the same girlfriend that always asked me how I always manage to find the good ones. My reply was, "By not being a bitch!"

Okay, ladies, now I know most women are looking for a successful man who is able to hold his own, but allow a relationship to progress naturally *before* you start making demands. I have had the pleasure of being involved with many successful men and I have found that when you allow a man the time to get to know and love you there is nothing he won't do for you. However, if you initially come across as trying to get into his pockets, he will quickly label you as a gold digger and will run in the opposite direction.

In some cases, it is harder for a woman to get into a committed relationship with a man simply because she has to try harder to earn his trust. Many men have had bad experiences with materialistic women who were only after him for what he could provide for her. Gold diggers are everywhere! Sometimes it doesn't even matter if a woman has her own money. Women with money may have acquired that money by being a gold digger. Men are a lot less trusting than women and some of them feel that they have more to lose. So it is perfectly normal for men to be extremely cautious when it comes to committing to a relationship. But let me tell you, once you earn that trust, a man will go to the end of the Earth for you.

Always carry yourself well and maintain a positive self-image that demonstrates self-confidence and an approachable demeanor.

Great relationships are built on of chemistry. Without attraction and chemistry, nothing happens. Chemistry is either there or it's not, but that shouldn't stop you from being nice to any man who approaches you in a respectful manner.

Understanding How Men Think

*S*omehow there is a misconception that men are not interested in commitment and they do not have a desire to communicate. But I beg to differ. Every week on my radio show there is an astounding number of men who call in to give their thoughts and opinions on our topics. Men admit to wanting love, romance, and marriage even more so than women. All of these elements are important to them. Although there is a vast difference in how women and men relate to each other, in retrospect, we ultimately want many of the same things. However, although we may want many of the same things we do not communicate our needs in the same way.

I'm not going to go so deep into the differences between men and women because if I did, it could end up being a book in itself. Besides, there have been enough *Men Are From Mars, Women Are From Venus* books written already. We already know that men and women are just different. Once we accept that difference we can move on and learn how to communicate with each other in a manner that allows the development of trust and intimacy.

Women have our own language in how we relate to each other. We can discuss an issue that for us may appear to be a life or death situation with our girlfriends, women family members, neighbors, and co-workers. We can discuss these issues with ease, and another woman can understand and relate to our problem. She may even offer advice that seems perfectly logical. But you can take that same issue to the man in your life and he might look at you as if you are speaking a foreign language, because to him you are!

It is possible to effectively communicate with a man, but women must first understand that men don't understand the same language that we use with other women. We can't expect men to want to discuss every single detail about every single issue that we find important. Men do not value the need to discuss and analyze every little thing. If he did, he wouldn't be a *MAN*; he would be called a *WOMAN*.

How many times have we heard (or spoken) the phrase *"All he thinks about is sex!"* This is another area in which women and men differ. Men express love through sex. They show love and affection through sex. Women express love through an emotional connection.

For example, I recall in a previous relationship after losing my job I was under an extreme amount of stress. It was difficult losing a part-time job working approximately three to four days a week where I earned a salary of $65,000.00 a year. So when I was laid off due to the decline in the economy, I found myself back in the job market again after fourteen years. Although I was doing quite well with my other business ventures, losing the 65K had a huge impact on my lifestyle. But what type of job could I possibly find that would compensate for the amount of money that I made at my previous job for the minimal amount of time that I worked? Most people could understand the amount of stress that I was under, but one night, I found myself needing that little extra attention. So I said to my man at the time, "Honey, I'm not in a good place right now, my life seems so uncertain and I just need to feel that you love me." Of course, he didn't reply but reached for me (and began to stroke my backside), which was his signal for initiating sex. Most men would respond in a similar fashion. Most men don't understand what a woman needs when she needs to feel loved. Most haven't been trained in the art of what it takes to make a woman *want* to engage in sex. They don't understand that running a bubble bath, giving her that back massage or massaging her scalp will encourage her to feel more romantic towards him.

He couldn't understand that had he encouraged me to talk about my feelings as he listened; it would have been enough to make me *want* to have sex with him.

When I saw where he was heading, I immediately said to him, "This is not about sex...sex can't fix everything!"

He replied in astonishment, "This wasn't about sex. I was just trying to make you feel good!" Men feel that by offering sex, he is giving you something. When there is a problem within the relationship they immediately react with sex, because sex is what works for him. When he comes home stressed from a hard day at work, he may want sex, because for him, sex relieves the tension and helps him to unwind. Sex also confirms to him that you love him and find him appealing. Sex reassures him of your love for him. Therefore, he feels by giving you sex, he is showing that he loves and cares about you.

Fortunately, this was a *previous* relationship and I consider myself blessed that I don't have this problem in my current relationship, but some women do.

This is why you must make that extra effort to communicate your needs to your partner without judging. Communication is one of the most important elements to having a successful relationship. When occasions such as the one noted above arises, instead of acting negatively and accusing him of not caring about your feelings, take a different approach. It may be necessary to take a deep breath and exhale before you respond. Taking this moment will allow you the opportunity to look at the situation from his point of view. Put yourself in his place. Chances are he's not intentionally reacting this way in order to hurt you. And because he is a man, he doesn't understand how you think. So, if he is just not getting it, don't get angry or let your frustration take precedent over rational thinking. Remember all of the wonderful things that you love about him. It requires the effort of two people in order to effectively communicate. Consider how you could better respond to what he considers "good intentions". If not, he could possibly shut down due to feelings of rejection or inadequacy.

Men experience emotions just as we do, although he may not display that side of himself to you. For him, it is much easier to shut down than it is to let you in. Both parties have to be receptive to openly communicating to address and resolve an issue. If only one party is willing, it is not communication; that is a one-sided conversation. Both parties have to be receptive to work through a conflict to reflect your commitment to each other. As long as there are relationships, conflicts will undoubtedly exist. Two people will never feel the same every day. So in order to learn how to resolve conflict, you must learn how to communicate in a way that your partner understands.

Lack of communication is a relationship killer. It was the primary factor that caused the demise of my second marriage. Although my second husband was a wonderful husband and provider he was a horrible communicator. He felt that anytime I needed to *feel* loved, I was asking for sex. I, on the other hand, couldn't understand why he couldn't react the way I needed him to. Why couldn't he come home and give me a detailed play-by-play report on how his day went, instead of replying, "It was fine." When we were experiencing problems, why couldn't *he* take *me* by the hand and lovingly talk it out? At that stage in my life, twenty-five years old and in my second marriage (it was his first), although I loved him and knew what I needed, I didn't understand how to communicate those needs to him in a manner that he understood. So rather than be patient and try to talk it out in order to *learn* what works, I decided to end the marriage. After all, he wasn't giving me what I needed. But I have found that when you don't take the time to connect on a deeper level, you will spend the rest of your life walking away from a relationship or marriage because you don't know how to communicate with each other. So it is best to learn how to communicate with your man.

When women have been away from our man all day we want to talk. When we ask, "Honey, how was your day?" we want the details. Isn't it funny that when our man comes home and asks us about our day, we will give him an up-to-the-minute report starting with the moment he left our sight? We tell him each and every little detail that happened during the day, right down to not being able to find a parking spot at the local supermarket. But men are just the opposite. When their work day ends the last thing they want to do is talk about it.

He doesn't want to talk about anything that has stressed him out during the day.

Most men have a short attention span, so when you have a problem, he would rather you tell him exactly what you need so he can fix it. He wants to get right to the point and not go through all of that unnecessary conversation. All he wants to know is, "What can I do to fix the problem?" So, before you give him that, "Honey, I think we need to talk" speech; make sure you are prepared to get right to the point.

Understand that men have a difficult time expressing their feelings, but they ultimately want the same things that we do, which is emotional support. Men enjoy and need emotional support, only they don't know how to ask for it, so continually praise your man for all the things he is doing right. Let him know that you find him super sexy and that you are proud to have him in your life. Remember, the male ego is a fragile thing. And if you can make your man feel like "the man" you will find that he will spend most of his time catering to you. He will make it his mission to make *you* happy.

It is common for people to love at different degrees. Nobody falls in love at the same level, or in many cases, even at the same time. At whatever point you realize that you love your man, it is okay to say so. However, do not press him to reciprocate those same feelings for you. Know that when he's ready, and his feelings for you are genuine, he will tell you that he loves you.

It is common for most women to anxiously look forward to hearing those three crucial words from her man. "I Love You!" Most women can remember the exact date and time that her man uttered those words to her, because for her it signifies the turning point in the relationship. This proves to her that her man is taking their relationship to the next level. It says that he trusts her enough to share his feelings with her. However, a woman shouldn't be fooled by every man that tells you he loves you. Sometimes men who are not interested in having a committed relationship will tell you this because he knows it is what you want to hear. So know the difference!

What Do Men Really Want?

How many times have women asked this question? Most men readily admit to wanting a woman who is physically attractive, so we know that physical attractiveness is at the top of the list. But this alone is not enough. Attractive, successful men often have more choices in terms of the women they can be with, so there has to be something that stands out about you *other* than attractiveness. There is one thing that I have always believed in, "A man will commit when he finds what he's looking for!" So your job is to know, or learn, what your man is looking for in a woman and a potential wife. This may require some observation, listening, and practical application because it's not easy to get a man to just tell you what he's looking for. It could be that he has problems verbalizing his wants or needs to you. He may not know what he wants or his needs may constantly change. Either way, it is up to you to decipher what he isn't saying. Recently, I sent out e-mails, bulletins, and posted on blogs asking men to give their honest opinion on exactly what they looked for in a woman. The information contained here came directly from those replies.

✓ **A sense of humor.**

Men love women who don't take themselves too seriously. Having a sense of humor is not only attractive, but it is vital to the existence of a good relationship. Men enjoy the company of women who are not afraid to let their hair down and have fun, even if it means getting dirty.

✓ **Beautiful inside, as well as out!**

Truly beautiful women recognize other beautiful women, so when you see another attractive woman smile, speak, and acknowledge her. A woman who is secure and recognizes her own beauty does not envy other attractive women. In addition, it displays self-confidence and class to your man. Even when it seems he is not paying attention he is always watching.

✓ **A woman who is independent!**

A man loves a woman who is capable of holding her own; whether it's financially or emotionally. He wants to *feel* needed and not have to *be* needed. A woman who is needy will only make him feel restricted and confined.

✓ **A woman who has her own identity and sense of self!**

One who enjoys life and is not dependent on him for her happiness. I always say have a life of your own other than the one you have with him. A woman should be strong and independent, not clingy and dependent. Have your own interests and hobbies. I truly love my man, however, I understand that he had goals and interests before he met me. I don't expect him to change who he is just to accommodate me. The reverse is also true for me. It makes me love him that much more when he allows me time to have my own life and to continue to pursue my dreams.

✓ Class!

Class is what sets you apart from the next woman. It is how you handle yourself in any situation that a man remembers most.

✓ Romance!

Believe it or not, men love to be romanced just as much as we do. It confirms the fact that he is never far from your mind. So do those special things for him just because—send those flowers to work, leave love notes in his briefcase to let him know that you are thinking of him.

✓ A woman who feeds his EGO!

Remember my number one rule. *The way to a man's heart is through his EGO!* When you make your man feel great about himself, during moments when life gets him down, he will come to you for reassurance; to make him feel better about himself, to make him feel like a man. You see what I mean? In many ways men are no different than women.

You have the ability to make your man feel like *SUPERMAN*. If you think I'm kidding, just try it. The next time he washes your car say to him, "Oh honey, my car is so clean. You're the best!" or when he mows the lawn say, "Oh baby, I have the nicest looking lawn in the neighborhood! I'm so happy!" I guarantee you he will beam with pride and joy because he was able to make you happy.

✓ **A woman who makes him feel special!**

You can never tell a man enough just how wonderful he is.

✓ **A woman who is not so overly focused on their relationship.**

Men do not want a woman who wants to discuss any little detail that deviates from the norm. If he fails even once to inform her that he will be late, she freaks out and accuses him of cheating.

✓ **A woman who can go from the boardroom to the bedroom!**

Someone he can take out in the public and never have to worry about her saying or doing anything that will embarrass him in front of his peers or business associates, but in an instant can transform into his sexual fantasy.

✓ **A woman who genuinely shares mutual interests.**

Although my man and I have separate goals, we also share mutual goals and interests. We're not only lovers; we make the best business partners. We're building an empire together.

✓ **A woman who enjoys SEX!**

Whoever said that sex is not important is WRONG! Men marry sexually captivating women.

Men fall in love through sex and women give up sex through love. Men can fall in love based off sex, but not just any sex will do; it has to be *good* sex. For a woman, sex is a way of displaying her emotional commitment to her man. For a man, sex is a physical act that satisfies that need for release and relieves the pressure caused by testosterone.

Every woman at some point has accused her man of *only* wanting sex, even me, but the fact is, if a man is into you and finds you desirable, he will want sex! The bottom line is that it doesn't necessarily mean that he *only* wants you for sex!

In order to get your man, you have to know what he wants. I've said it before; men fall in love based off sex. So give him what he wants; mind-blowing SEX!

Let's Talk About SEX!

kay ladies, we have established how men feel about sex. Sex is one of a man's basic needs. Sometimes, their minds are constantly preoccupied with thoughts about sex throughout a day. It doesn't matter what his day consists of, sex is never far from his mind. He can have a big project due at work, yet he will still find time to think of sex. As I said earlier, it is the one thing that is never far from their minds and I have never met a man who has refused or had no interest in sex. But on the flip side of that, it is important to recognize that sex alone will not get him to put that ring on your finger.

One important thing to remember when it comes to sex, is that *you* are in control. A man can only connect with you sexually if you allow him to. Women will always have that power over a man. Unfortunately, some women abuse that power. Some women use sex as a bargaining tool. It's a big taboo that men feel that women give it up initially to get him, but as the relationship progresses, men claim that women tend to withhold sex or ration sexual favors in order to get what she wants.

Ladies, we need intimacy, men need sex! Withholding sex from your man is like giving him a license to cheat. Most men have admitted to me that they cheat because of a lack of passion in their relationship. Lackluster sex is simply not enough. A man wants passion, he wants to feel wanted. And I'm not talking about just going to bed and letting him have his way with you. No man wants a woman who just lies there. This behavior will make him feel that you don't desire him. Never make your man feel that you do not desire sex with him, and never under any circumstance say to a man, "Hurry up and get it over with!" I don't care how tired you are, or how early you may have to get up the next morning. No matter how you say these words to a man they are going to hurt. All he hears is that you don't desire him and for you, making love to him is not pleasurable. He may even feel that you don't find him physically appealing anymore. In any case, these are words that should never be spoken to a man you love.

It is understandable that sometimes you're tired. Life itself is exhausting. You have worked all day, now you have to go home and take care of the kids. By the time dinner is prepared, homework is done, and all the kids are finally in bed, now he wants some of your time and you feel like you have absolutely nothing left to give. I do understand when women tell me this. One of my readers, who is now a very good friend, contacted me via MySpace wanting to know how was it possible to balance an active sex life while working full-time and taking care of five kids. Well, I don't have any children, but I do work two jobs and still have to find time to run my business, but you know what? I have a wonderful man. And although I have a full plate it is not fair to him for me to force him to take a back seat to everything else in my life when he is so good to me. So, I'll share *my* secret with you.

When I'm really tired and know my man wants intimacy, I never neglect him. I will throw on my sexiest lingerie, strap on some killer stilettos and enter the bedroom ready for action. I may whisper in his ear, "Baby, I'm tired, but I want you so badly. I really need to feel you inside me tonight. Let's have a quickie tonight."

This always works, and talking dirty to your man further enhances his stimulation and makes him even more eager. You are encouraging him not to hold back. By telling him you want a quickie, it releases him from the obligation of trying to hold out until you get yours. He is excited because you are already ready. Now when I suggest this to women they sometimes come back to say that their bodies won't respond if they're not in the mood. Now I do understand that for some women it takes time to get turned on, but sometimes we all need that little extra help. I have one word for you, ladies — ASTROGLIDE! Astroglide is a life and relationship saver! It's not gummy and sticky like some personal lubricants. Its silkiness gives you that extra sensation that may quickly put you in the mood, even when you're not. It's even possible to use and your man doesn't even have to know that it's not your own natural wetness. Who said we can't be superwoman? All it takes is a little planning and imagination. A sexually fulfilled man is a happy man and a happy man is one who will always cater to you. So muster up some energy and give your *good* man some *exceptional* loving!

Now, although I don't believe in withholding sex, I do feel that in certain situations it is appropriate to shut down *the goody box!* Some men look at sex as a given. He thinks his woman is automatically supposed to give it up just because you are "in a relationship." But there are times when a man must "earn" sexual privileges. As I stated earlier, if you are in a situation where you need assistance or support of any sort and your man is not providing that support, he is not deserving of twenty-four hour sexual favors. But if your man is the total package, holding it down, taking care of home, why wouldn't you want to cater to his needs?

Understand what your man really wants. Knowing and meeting your partner's needs is a primary part of intimacy. Men are basically simple and don't require a lot, but they all have their basic needs and most of the time it's SEX! If its sex that drives him, make your sexual encounters something he will remember every time. If he enjoys waking up to oral sex every morning, you have got to be willing to do that (well...maybe not *every* morning but you get the idea). If it's food that he's into, you'd better be Martha Stewart in the kitchen (preferably nude and in five inch heels). Keeping your man interested in you is essential to the survival of your relationship.

No matter what you engage in, it's all about variety, so be creative and have fun! There are so many tools available on the market today to ensure that sex is never dull or boring.

A woman should be able to bring her man to orgasm by three methods.

1. Intercourse
2. Orally
3. Masturbation (also known as a good old fashioned hand job.)

And, ladies, if you know of any other methods I'm sure your man will appreciate those as well, but for now we'll talk about these three primary methods.

• Intercourse~ One of the greatest things about sexual intercourse is that it can provide women with the intimacy that we crave in our relationships. It gives us the opportunity to connect with our partner on a deeper emotional level. During intercourse you are accepting him—the one you love— into your essence. There is nothing more powerful than that. Whether you know it or not, most men are most vulnerable during intercourse. He is able to let his guards down, release that macho exterior and truly *cling* to his woman. But he wants you to be just as uninhibited.

• Oral sex~ One of the primary complaints that I hear from men is that their woman doesn't enjoy, or is not willing, to perform oral sex to his satisfaction.

I had a conversation recently, with a man who claims that his wife is sexually repressed.

"She doesn't want me to go down on her because she thinks it's gross. She doesn't enjoy sex at all...so, in order to get her to do it, I have to go out and buy her some outrageously expensive gift. And then she only gives me repayment sex," he said. "She repays me for my expensive gifts by just lying there and letting me have my way with her. She always has this bored expression on her face and I can tell she really just wants me to hurry up and get it over with." He paused for a moment and then continued, "Asking her to go down on me is out of the question. That has only happened twice in the four years that we have been married. Then she runs to the bathroom and drinks a bottle of mouthwash."

I laughed, because I thought this was funny, yet, it is one of the common complaints that men express about the women in their lives.

Ladies, one of the greatest sexual acts for a man is oral sex. Men love the feel of a woman's mouth on his manhood, even if she's not good at it. Men define "not good at it" as a lack of enthusiasm. However, being good at performing oral sex requires skill, and all it takes to develop that skill is listening and a willingness to learn. There is an art to being good at orally satisfying a man. However, if you don't enjoy it, you better believe your man will know. So, in order to keep your man sexually fulfilled, don't just *act* like you enjoy it, *learn* to enjoy it.

Every man is different, so what feels good to one may not be quite as enjoyable to another, so ask your man what feels good to him. Orally pleasuring my man is a definite turn-on for me. I can't teach you to love it, but I can teach you how to make it pleasurable for you as well as for him.

One of the most important things about performing oral sex is making sure that you are in a comfortable position, especially if you are fortunate enough to have a well-endowed man. Position your body so that he can watch you pleasuring him. Men find it exciting to watch as his manhood disappears into your mouth. Let your expression show that there is nowhere else you would rather be at that moment. Do not approach fellatio in a manner of it being a chore. Be flirty, playful, and tease him with your tongue, your eyes, your hands and even your hair. Every man wants to feel that his woman worships his member, so gaze into his eyes as you run your tongue over the head of his penis. Let him see how much you enjoy it. Don't feel disappointed or inadequate if you cannot take all of him in your mouth. As long as you display unsurpassed enthusiasm for what you are doing, your man will be happy!

• Masturbation~ some men enjoy manual stimulation, also referred to as a good, old-fashioned hand job.

Being with a woman who knows how to bring him pleasure in this way enhances his attraction to her. Masturbation works in two ways. Ladies, first you have to know that men are going to masturbate with or without you! The quicker you understand and accept this fact, the better off you will be. There are a large number of women who have contacted me to express some form of displeasure or resentment because she doesn't understand her man's need to masturbate. Just because your man chooses to masturbate does not mean that he is not pleased with your sexual encounters. It doesn't mean that there is something you are not doing to pleasure him. He's just being a man and doing what men do. Men grew up masturbating from the time they were boys and I have never met a man who says he doesn't do it. Think about it this way, would you rather he sneak off and do it, or would you appreciate him allowing you to be a part of the experience by openly pleasuring himself in front of you without fear of being chastised by you? Personally, I'll take the latter.

I am so fortunate because my man is extremely sexual. He doesn't hide any of his desires from me because he trusts me. He also knows when it comes to intimacy with him I am usually game for whatever. We enjoy each other fully and nothing turns me on more than watching him pleasure himself. Likewise, I will often masturbate in front of my man. I get off on the expression on his face. Masturbating in front of your man shows him what you like and how you like to be touched. Men are highly visual, and this act can only lead to him learning about what you enjoy and what you want.

In the past, I could tell a man until I was blue in the face what I wanted and how I wanted it. (I'm definitely not a shy woman.) I could even take his hand and guide it to the spot and show him how I wanted to be touched. But as soon as I released his hand, within a few minutes he'd be right back to jabbing and grinding his fingers inside me like he was searching for gold! OUCH!

It's amazing how after I pleasured myself in front of him, his whole approach changed. Later, I asked him why the change? He said, "You never had such a powerful orgasm with me as you did when you did it yourself. I had to learn because I couldn't let you outdo me!"

As I said, allow your man to watch and learn.

Another aspect of capturing and maintaining a man's interest is keeping ourselves together at all times. Always be fresh, clean and well-groomed. Good personal hygiene is a must! Practice good sexual health. Be sure to make regular appointments for checkups, especially after ending a sexual relationship. It is always a good idea to get checked out before becoming sexually involved with a new partner, even if you practiced safe sex.

A little excitement goes a long way. Some of you need to swim your way up out of that sexual rut. There are so many ways to revive a struggling sex life. There are visual aids, toys, sexual enhancement creams, jellies, gels and board games.

You name it, the possibilities are endless. Don't be afraid to have fun. After all, this is the man that you love.

My man's job takes him out of the country quite frequently. Before his return from one of his most recent trips, he called me and said he wanted me to meet his plane at the airport in a raincoat and nothing else. We had a good laugh about it, but the truth was, I couldn't wait to see him and the raincoat idea was right up my alley.

However, it was mid-September, one of the hottest months of the summer, so I tried to think of the next best thing. I ran to the mall and purchased this ultra sexy, red wrap dress and paired it with a pair of five inch stilettos. This dress was form-fitting and it hugged every curve of my body; leaving nothing to the imagination. The appreciative look on his face as he walked into the lobby of the airport was priceless. To top that, the look on the rest of his crew's face was that of total envy. Especially when they were being greeted by their plain-Jane girlfriend's and wives. Obviously, he had already let the rest of his crew in on the joke, since one of his co-workers asked, "Where's the raincoat?" I did a sexy spin and replied, "This is it!" You have to imagine the picture I painted with that statement; they all knew I was completely nude under my dress. As I said, it's all about having fun and being creative.

Knowing and meeting your partner's needs is a primary part of intimacy. But there may be instances where your man may ask you to participate in sexual acts that you are not comfortable with. If this is the case, be straightforward and tell him how you feel.

For example, usually, I am not an anal girl! I have tried anal sex in the past, not particularly because I was interested in it, but because my partner seemed to have an interest in it. I

found that it did nothing for me. But I have found that some
men seem to be fascinated with it. For the life of me, I can't
even begin to tell you why it is so appealing to them. Some say
that it's adventurous and something different, sort of like
forbidden fruit. However, most men don't realize the magni-
tude of what they are asking you to do, and over the years, I
developed my own way of discouraging my sexual partners
should they suggest we try this act. I would say to my partner,
"If I can do you with a dildo that is equivalent to the size of
your penis, then I'll allow you to do me." Now, as soon as you
suggest this to most men, they immediately change their
minds and are no longer interested. This has worked for me.
But if your man is insisting you try something that you are not
comfortable with, don't just do it to pacify him. Don't allow
anyone to talk you into performing *any* sexual act that you are
not comfortable with. If you do, your partner may come to
expect you to perform this act and you will eventually begin to
resent him for asking you to do it. Resentment has no place in
a relationship, it spreads like a cancer and it only needs to be
prevalent in one of you to manifest itself.

Now, ladies, I know that many of you are not pleased with
the sex life you have with your partner. Yet, because we worry
about damaging a man's fragile ego, sometimes we suffer in
silence. Many women have never had an orgasm during
intercourse, so they fake it. In my earlier years, I, too, have
faked orgasms. However, many years ago I came to the
realization that by faking an orgasm I was only hurting
myself. Ladies, when we fake orgasms we cheat ourselves.
Although a man's ego is fragile, I think it's important to let
him know what you're feeling. If he's not doing it for you, it's
only fair that you say so. After all, you're part of the relation-

ship and your feelings count for something too. You deserve pleasure! You must find a way to address your sexual issues in a loving manner that will not damage his, or your, self-esteem.

I don't want women to get the wrong idea about this book and think that it is all about pleasing your man. It's not! It is about taking responsibility for the woman that you are, and your feelings about sex should be just as important to him as his are to you.

It's funny, but during one of my radio shows one of my callers said that he's always amazed at how little women actually know about their bodies. Some don't know the vagina from the clitoris or the vulva. He went on to express that some women don't even know how these parts actually work in bringing pleasure. I had to admit that he was right. I have often had this discussion with women as well. This is why it's important to get to know your body. Therefore, I'm going to break this next lesson down for you.

When it comes to our bodies, we have a very limited area to work with. Sometimes a man can touch us and accidentally get it right, but there is a huge difference when it comes to a man's anatomy. A man's genital area is more extensive than ours, so keep in mind that what works for one man may not work for the next. If your last man enjoyed having the head of his penis stroked, your current man may require something different. Ladies, the easiest way to identify what your man wants is to ask him. Do not assume anything!

I had a conversation with a young lady who claimed that she couldn't bring her man to orgasm by manual stimulation. She asked me what she was doing wrong. My reply was, "Well, I don't know. What did he say?"

She replied, "Well, I didn't ask him."

So I tried a different approach and asked, "How do you know when your man is enjoying what you're doing?"

She said, "I go by his reaction. He tenses up and makes these groaning noises."

So I asked her, "When your man does something during sex that is unpleasant to you, what do you do?"

She replied, "I tense up and make unpleasant sounds."

I think she began to see my point when I asked, "When you're giving him manual stimulation, is it possible that you may have misinterpreted those groans of pain as moans of pleasure? So why not just ask him to show you how he'd like to be touched?"

She then said, "Well, I guess you're right!"

Ladies, let me tell you a story. In a previous relationship I couldn't bring my man to orgasm orally. I tried everything and because I couldn't do it, it was beginning to get on my nerves. So, one day as he and I were watching television, I said, sweetly, "You know, honey, I really enjoy making love to you. It's such a turn on for me when you have an orgasm and I want to be able to pleasure you orally. Show me what does it for you; tell me what you want me to do more of."

He put down his paper, took off his glasses and looked at me like he'd never seen me before and said, "I love you so much more right now. Most women wouldn't even care enough to ask."

From that point on, whenever I pleasured him orally—and when I did something that he enjoyed—he would encourage me to do more of it. We got beyond that barrier simply by talking about it. It's easy to please your man when you know what he wants.

Now there is a flip side to that too. A twenty-nine year old woman contacted me a few months ago. She was concerned because it appeared that her forty year old man was extremely inexperienced with sex. His sexual experiences were limited to what he had with his late wife. She had been his first and only sexual partner. This young lady was just the opposite. She was very sexual and had been with several other men. She wanted to encourage her man to try new things with sex, so she went out and bought some adult videos and a few toys, so that they could experiment. Although her partner tried to accommodate her, she could always tell he really wasn't into the experimental thing. As a result, he started being argumentative right before it was time to go to bed. She suspected that he would start arguments so he wouldn't have to try to have sex with her.

Ladies, sometimes you may have to understand that your sexual experiences may far surpass your man's, and although your man may still enjoy sex with you, when you push him to try new things he may feel that you are not happy with him. This can cause tension in your relationship. If you are with an inexperienced man who doesn't appear open to trying new things, you have to make some important decisions. Do you stay in the relationship and adapt, or do you find someone more compatible with you?

Finding Mr. Right!

hen my girlfriend Lydia's marriage ended, she often asked me, "Where do I go to meet men?" This is a question that I'm asked quite frequently by single women. Ladies, men are all around us. All we need to do is open our eyes to new experiences and opportunities. Stop going out looking for someone and just enjoy your daily activities. You may find Mr. Right in unlikely places—the post office, supermarket, or your local Home Depot. I have even met men at service stations, auto supply stores, car washes and even while stopped at a traffic light. Men are all around us, we don't have to go out shopping for them. However, if you do want to get out, hang out where men hang out; at the gym and at sporting events. Be cautious of hanging out in clubs or bars looking for someone to get into a long-term relationship with. Normally, when men frequent these places they are looking for a good time, not a future wife.

More likely than not, if you follow the advice above, and let your body language show that you are approachable, men will come to you.

Several months ago I was contacted by a twenty-four year old woman from Atlanta who asked, "How is it possible to find a man in a city like Atlanta where the ratio of women to men is twenty to one? How is it possible to find a man when you are dealing with those odds?"

I have spent quite a bit of time in the Atlanta area, as well as other cities and I am always amazed when women say that they can't find a man in a city like that. I have done some research and I'm still not sure of the actual ratio of women to men in Atlanta, but I can tell you about my experience on my most recent visit to Atlanta with three of my girlfriends.

Upon arriving in the city, we stopped to do some shopping at a busy strip mall. Within the first thirty minutes of our arrival, I was approached in a very respectful manner on four different occasions by four professional looking men who were interested in having a conversation with me. Because I'm always fascinated when women claim that they can't find a man in a city like Atlanta; I decided to do a study. After a brief conversation with each man, I disclosed that I am an author who writes about relationships and asked if they would participate in a survey by answering a few questions. They were more than willing to participate. I asked each man his age, occupation, (because I wanted to determine his economic level), whether he was married or single, what he looks for when he initially meets a lady and why he chose to approach me versus my other friends or other women who were in the immediate area. Here are the results:

1.   Thirty-three year old, automobile salesman, divorced, looks for a woman who smiles, the manner in which she carries herself, and her body language. He approached me because I made eye contact, my smile was genuine, I walked with confidence, and my body language made him feel he could approach me without getting cursed out.

2. Twenty-six-year old, hustler (his words, not mine), single, looks for a woman who is sure of herself and well-built. Especially if she appears nice. He approached me because I smiled, he liked my swagger (my walk), I had the sexiest legs he'd ever seen, and because I looked friendly, he could tell I wasn't from Atlanta.

3. Thirty-eight year old, insurance salesman, divorced, looks for a woman who is not too into herself, one who is attractive and takes care of her appearance and she has to have a great personality. He approached me because when he spoke to me, I actually smiled and spoke back. He listened to me laugh with my girlfriends and liked the sound of it, and I carried myself with confidence. Everything about me was sexy.

4. Forty-one year old, physical therapist, single (but has a live-in girlfriend), looks for a woman who is well put together, self assured, carries herself well. He approached me because he found me extremely attractive and as we walked past when he spoke to me, I made eye contact, smiled and said hello in a friendly voice. I looked happy and comfortable hanging with my friends, so he decided to approach me.

I was so amazed at the similarities of each man's comment. They all commented on my smile, the fact that I made eye contact, and the fact that I looked approachable. Number 1 and 2 made comments that I found a little strange, so, I asked man number 1 what he meant when he said he felt like he could approach me without getting cursed out. He said beautiful women in Atlanta know they're beautiful and they have an attitude like, "Why are you even speaking to me?" I asked man number 2 what he meant when he said he could tell I wasn't from Atlanta. He replied, "If you speak to a woman from Atlanta, most of the time she'll ignore you. If she does speak to you, she won't look at you and she won't smile." Number 4 actually pointed out one woman in the store and said, "Look at her. You can see her attitude from here!"

I do studies like this all the time; this was just to show that there are plenty of eligible attractive men all around us. Out of these four men, three of them claimed to be single, with the exception of number 4 who admitted to being in a committed relationship. Much of the problem appears that most men don't feel comfortable approaching some women without getting a negative response. Now, I will be the first to admit that in many cases you will meet men who portray themselves as single when they are actually married or seeing several different women. But as I said earlier, if you look at the situation for what it is you can quite easily see when someone is not being honest with you. You have more control than you think when it comes to men trying to play you.

Stop helping a man lie to you! Most of you remember the scene in the movie *Waiting to Exhale* where Robin (played by Lela Rochon) was reflecting on her relationship with Russell (played by Leon). In the clip, she was talking about her experience with Russell the night before. She said that they had such amazing sex, but that he couldn't stay the night. Then she continued, "He wanted to stay all night. And he would have, but he had to get up early to take his mama to church the next morning!"

This was funny because she was so gullible, but in all actuality these are the kind of lies that we tell ourselves to make ourselves feel better about a man's behavior. I stopped making excuses for men a long time ago. It is an easy process to get caught up in. A man might tell us something that we know doesn't make sense, but not only will we let it slide, some of us will *help* him make his lies make sense—because we know if we knew the truth we would have to do something about it.

When you give a man your number and he can't call you but he can *text* you, there should be a red flag waving in your face. I met my current man several years ago where we worked in the same building. We passed each other for years and never did more than speak a polite hello as we checked each other out. Ironically, six years later when we were both no longer working for the same company, he found me on one of my networking sites. When he messaged me for the first time he asked if I would like to go out to dinner or a movie someday, but *only* if I was single.

I was so impressed because most men don't care whether you are single, dating or married, and he did. Fortunately, I was single. I found his profile to be impressive. There weren't any half nude women on his page and I also noticed that there weren't any salacious, flirty comments either. Although his profile said he was single when he contacted me, I *knew* he was single. He gave me his cell number, home number and work number. He also assured me that it was okay to call him on any of the numbers anytime. This is when you know a man is not interested in playing games with you. He's being real.

Online dating seems to be a growing trend these days. Being that I do a lot of online networking, I am frequently approached by single men. I have never personally done the dating sites, but as a part of my research for one of the topics on my radio show, I did go on to several dating sites just to see what the appeal was and why people would pay money to find love.

I was amazed at what I actually found on some people's profiles. One man admitted that he was living with genital herpes and wanted to disclose it upfront, so that any woman interested would already know. One lady admitted that she was certifiably crazy and she was looking for a man (or a woman) to take care of her financially.

I was so amazed by what I found on those sites I had to question, is this what the world has evolved into? We can log on and actually shop for a person who fits what we are looking for, just as we would when purchasing a pair of shoes?

I do realize that for many people, online dating is an option. However, just as in real life face-to-face encounters, you have to be careful about what you are getting into. When you have the anonymity of the Internet you can be anyone you chose to be, so before getting caught up, do a background check to see if the person you are interested in is really who he claims to be.

When you finally meet that special someone that you could possibly be interested in, you have the right to know what you're getting into. So when you meet that someone there are a few mandatory questions that *must* be asked. Are you single? This means not married, not in a relationship of any sort, not even with your baby's mama. Do you have children? What is your profession? I do feel that it's some-what impolite to come right out and ask a man what kind of work he does, but you can always say something like, "I am currently working as an administrative assistant (or whatever your job is), what kind of work do you do?"

I'll be perfectly honest when I tell you I don't want to waste my time with a man who doesn't want anything out of life. If that makes somebody label me a gold digger, then so be it, but if you approach the subject in this manner, the only man who will label you a gold digger is the one who doesn't have anything, so you're better off anyway.

The most important thing you should know about a man before becoming involved in a committed relationship or marriage is if he is trustworthy. You determine this by observing his actions. This won't happen overnight, but over a period of time. Watch how he relates to others as this can also teach you a lot about him. Observe his behavior in different surroundings. Does he have any friends? Does he get along with his co-workers? All of these things will help you determine a man's true character.

Remember, every woman can find "Mr. Right-Now". However, when you are involved with Mr. Right-Now, it can sometimes cause you to become distracted. You may overlook Mr. Right due to your preoccupation with Mr. Right-Now. So learn to enjoy being solo until your Mr. Right comes along.

Why Should He Choose You?

*A*nyone who is familiar with me and my writing knows that I avidly preach how important it is to make a list of what your requirements are for a man. Make a list of standards that you expect in your man and be realistic. Now, I want you to apply the same principles to yourself. Make a list of your qualities and what would make a man want to be in a long-term committed relationship or marriage with you. Include in your list all the things that make you who you are and make you an asset to your partner. Simply ask yourself, "Why would any man choose me? What major strengths and attributes do I bring to the relationship?" I always hear from women who are looking for a good man, but what about what he's looking for, and what makes you it? What can you provide that he can't find in the next woman? This is a very real question. Make a list of the things that would make you an asset to your man.

For example, my list includes: I am an author, publisher and CEO of several different companies. I am a friend, mentor, motivational speaker and business consultant. I am a caregiver to those who cannot care for themselves. I am intelligent, witty, sexy as hell, and compassionate. Wow! Can you tell I love myself? I have so much to offer to a man as his partner.

Being an asset is about more than just being able to hold your own financially. We all contribute to our relationships in different ways. Maybe your man has no problems being the sole breadwinner and you both have made the decision that you will be the primary caregiver of the children. If this is the case, being the best mother, caregiver, and homemaker is your contribution to the relationship. If your contribution is being your man's best friend, then be that. Be his confidant, be his cheerleader. But whatever your role is, make sure you are the best at it. Now, let's take this one step further. No matter your role, always have a backup plan. If you are the homemaker and for some reason your relationship ends, what would you do? These are necessary questions you must ask and have a plan for just in case. I always feel that it is best to have some means of financial support because it allows you some independence.

I'm sure most everyone will agree that relationships can be complicated. You have to be willing to give 100% at all times. If not, chances are there will be problems. Contrary to what most people believe, relationships and marriages are not 50/50, but it is about balance. Over the course of relationships, events happen. There could be an illness, loss of a job, death in the family; any number of things could happen that could take your relationship on a brand-new course. If your man lost his job, you may have to chip in 100% while he gives nothing. At any moment, the roles could reverse. Which why I say in a committed relationship or marriage you must be willing to give at least 100% at all times.

Things You Should Do

✓ **Spend as much time as possible in his home.**

By doing this, you are allowing him to become accustomed to your presence in his home. If he associates your presence with pleasant experiences, he will realize how much he misses and appreciates you when you are not there.

✓ **Love his buddies.**

No, don't literally *love* his buddies, but his friends are going to help you get your man. They will be there to validate your *fineness* to him every opportunity they get. I never turn down the opportunity to go to a cookout, party, bonfire, or any other event around his family, friends and co-workers. When you are around his circle of friends, make sure you are always on point and at your most fabulous. Your man may not say anything, but he will get a kick out of watching other men watch you. It will make him proud to have other men lusting after what is his alone. So, be sure to attend those social gatherings with him, and never neglect the opportunity to cement yourself in his life. If nothing, else it shows that you are supportive.

✓ **Do not force yourself on his children.**

Allow them space and the opportunity to get to know you at their own pace. Kids are not dumb, so don't try to buy them or bribe them to get in their good graces.

✓ **Flirt with your man.**

Many women complain that when they go out in public, other women (cocktail waitresses, servers, bartenders...etc.,) flirt with their man. One way of avoiding this, is to flirt with him yourself.

You see, when I go out to a restaurant with my man, rather than sit across from him; I prefer to sit next to him. This way he can get all of my attention. I might rub on his thigh under the table, whisper in his ear, and lay my head on his shoulder — who knows. I am the queen of flirting, and who better to flirt with than my man? Trust me, when you have his attention, there is no way he will notice if another woman even *attempts* to flirt with him! And remember, you're never too old to flirt.

Flirting in general is fun, stimulating, and a huge ego-booster. It is also harmless. Just because you flirt does not mean that you are trying to get with someone. But many women admit that they don't know how to flirt. Flirting is easy! Being a natural at it comes with developing confidence. Once you have that level of confidence you will be able to hold your head high, make eye contact and smile.

Okay ladies, now I know this one is going to be hard to absorb.

✓ **Know when to shut up and let your man be a man! Allow a man to be nice to you.**

Real men enjoy doing nice things for a woman he cares for. Let him be a man and do those things. Sometimes women get so caught up in trying to prove our independence to men that we forget how important it is for men to do nice things for us. So sit back and enjoy being treated special. After all, we deserve it!

✓ **Tame your inner green-eyed monster.**

As humans, insecurities are bound to become visible sometime during the course of a relationship. This is why being able to trust your partner is so important. When you have that level of trust, you know your partner would never do anything to hurt you or jeopardize your relationship and it will be easier to suppress that green-eyed monster.

✓ **No drama...please!**

A few weeks ago on my radio show, our topic was "Hooked on DRAMA!" I was amazed at the number of men who actively participated in this discussion. Most men agreed that they try to live their lives as drama-free as possible. They also admitted that they would not commit to a woman who displayed signs of emotional instability. So ladies, if you know that you are emotionally out of control, you also know that most men will stay as far away from you as possible. I know some men who are so determined to avoid drama they won't even watch reality television.

Speaking of reality television, during the show, some men felt that women are watching too much of the wrong things when it comes to reality television programs. Many men felt that some of these programs can give some women—who do not have the mental capacity to see it for what it is—a distorted view of reality. I had to disagree with certain points some of the guys made, simply because I think some reality television is entertaining. But it should be just that, ENTERTAINMENT!

✓ **Make your man your priority.**

Notice I never said anything about being a doormat. But if you have a good man, who exhibits good qualities, he deserves your time, attention and affection. For example, give a proper greeting at the end of the day. Make your man want to come home to you.

One guy explained that he hates to go home at the end of the day and would often go to the local bar for happy hour with his friends before going home to his woman. He claims that he would do anything to delay having to go home to his woman. She normally greeted him at the door with her hands on her hips and an attitude that had been festering all day. So, before he goes home and listens to her nag, he'd rather have a few drinks in order to numb the pain that's sure to greet him as he walks through the door.

✓ **Some men feel unappreciated in their relationships.**

Recently, I was contacted by a male who said to me, "I don't feel my woman appreciates me. When I arrive home, she doesn't give me the proper greeting that I expect. Yesterday, I walked in as she was vacuuming the floor. She came so close to me that the vacuum actually bumped my shoe, but instead of reaching over and giving me a kiss, she finished the entire room before she even looked up and acknowledged that I was there. Where is the love in that?"

Ladies, never fail to give your man what he needs. This is how so many men end up having affairs. When he doesn't get the attention that he craves from you—his woman—he will turn to someone else for that attention. It doesn't make it right, but it happens.

✓ Men have huge egos. Stroke it!

There are those who believe in the old saying "The way to a man's heart is through his stomach." However, I believe that the way to a man's heart is through his *ego*, so stroke it! Ladies, you have the power to make your man feel like Superman!

✓ Reward your man!

When your man goes out of his way to do something special for you let him know that you appreciate him. Don't take the things that he does for granted. If you have a good man and you know it, then do the things that he asks of you. There is one thing I have always told my man, "I will never tell you 'no'." If he asks me to do something that is not going to hurt me, hurt someone else or break any laws, I'll do it. Simply because I know I have a wonderful, exceptional man and he deserves exceptional treatment. So, ladies, try it out. Never say no. I only suggest this if you have a *good* man. I wouldn't do this for just *any* man.

✓ Learn to have a love affair with yourself by making time for you!

A woman who is relaxed is better able to deal with the stresses of everyday life. So, take some time to pamper yourself. It could be as simple as indulging in a bubble bath, massage or facial.

✓ Know how to read a man's body language and personality!

Learning to read a man's body language and personality comes with getting to know him better. This is one area you will learn more about as the relationship progresses. But keep in mind—because we're human—we're going to make mistakes along the way. A smart person learns from those mistakes, and sometimes, you must be the bigger person and admit when you've messed up.

✓ Don't be pushy!

No matter how anxious you are to have your man commit, do not press the issue. However, do stand up for yourself and say, "I'm looking for a relationship. I do not believe in casual sex and I can't be your casual sex buddy!" By making a stand, you are making it clear what your needs are. Word of advice, do this during the early stages of a relationship, not after you have been seeing and sleeping with each other for months.

✓ **When you say something MEAN IT!**

If not, you lose your credibility. If you say you will not tolerate infidelity, yet you continue to stay when you catch your man cheating, you lose your credibility. He knows you are not going anywhere and will continue with the bad behavior.

✓ **The most important rule of all.** *Treat your man like "the" man!*

Men are not much different than women in many aspects. They love preferential treatment. So, when you're with your man, never treat him indifferently, show him that you care. Make him feel like he matters and never under any circumstance take him for granted.

✓ **Know the difference between love and control!**

There are times when we are convinced that a man loves us. I have been in this situation and if you don't look at the situation carefully, you could confuse control for love. There are varying degrees of control.

Some women don't know what signs to look for in a man who wants (and expects) total control, so I will address some of the signs you should look for to determine if you are with a controlling man.

The most obvious sign of control is if he shows signs of anger when things don't immediately go his way. A man who desires control is one who is happy as long as he feels he is winning all the time. If at some point you say or do anything that goes against what he wants, he will become upset, use profanity, throw things or slam doors. He does these things to get your attention and he is only at his best when things are going his way. He may display possessiveness and jealousy when you do something that doesn't include him. He will often try to convince you why you shouldn't spend time with your friends and family. When he is angry he will often be disrespectful, say mean or hateful things. He may even attempt to control the choices and behavior of others around him, even at work. He may be impatient and easily irritated. He may have a hard time relaxing, and on weekends and holidays he may be convinced that he has to constantly be doing something. He doesn't feel worthy unless he is doing something that is going to create order. He hates being told what to do; he is domineering and overly critical. He can also become violent.

It is hard to live with someone who is a control freak. I know because I have been there. You may try to do everything you can in order to keep the peace, but remember that no one deserves to be controlled.

If the man you are in a relationship with displays any of the signs above, you are indeed in a controlling relationship. It may be necessary for you to re-evaluate your relationship. You should recognize that you deserve someone in your life that will treat you with love and respect at all times, even when they are angry.

✓ **Be passionate about something!**

Whatever it is that you do in life, do it with pride!

✓ **Get a life!**

Many women feel insecure when their men have outside interests that don't include them. But everyone needs their own space in a relationship. It's okay to have shared interests, but encourage your man to have his own interests that don't include you. I know it sounds harsh, but while women want to have that feeling of togetherness with their partner, you must understand that even though your man has his own interests, it doesn't mean that he doesn't love you. In order for love to grow it needs breathing room.

A man recently came to me with this complaint: If he went out with the boys, his girlfriend would sit at home pouting and waiting for his return. She would frequently call throughout the night and make him feel guilty for leaving her home all alone. Ladies, this is definitely one way of losing your man. Don't smother him, give him that breathing room. Find you a hobby or something to occupy your time during your time apart.

✓ **Sex, sex, and more sex please!**

Be sexually spontaneous! Do something out of the ordinary to make your man think of you.

For example: A man that I was in a relationship with asked me to attend his friend's retirement party with him. We had a great time at the party, dancing, and having fun being in each other's company. On the way home, we were making out in the car at every traffic light. We couldn't keep our hands off each other and we couldn't wait to get home and ravish each other. When we arrived at his house I took my thong and slipped it over the gear shift in his vehicle without him noticing. Needless to say, once behind closed doors we had a night filled with passion.

The next day, he went out to a fast food restaurant to pick up lunch. He discovered my thong as he arrived at the drive thru window. Of course he called me and I could hear him saying excitedly to the guy at the drive thru window, "Hey look, I've got panties!" The point is something so simple made his day and it also turned him on so much that when he got home he was ready for MORE action!

✓ **Keep a clean home.**

Men are most comfortable in clean environments. If your home is filthy, your man may not say anything but he notices. Always look at your home through a visitor's eyes. Walk in your home and take a look at your surroundings as if you were visiting for the first time. In our own homes we may become accustomed to seeing things out of order, but when you put yourself in the place of a visitor, you can see the things that detract away from the overall appearance of your home.

Look at light fixtures because they commonly hold dust, especially ceiling fans. Pay attention to pet odors. This is a biggie, because it is easy to get accustomed to how our home smells. Years ago, I worked as a real estate agent and frequently took clients to view homes. It's so amazing how a home can smell and the owners may not even be aware of it. Carpeting and furniture hold onto smells, especially if you have pets. I once walked into a woman's home that had twenty-one cats that all lived inside. Talk about odor!

My biggest pet peeve is a filthy bathroom. When I go into a person's home the first thing that I look at is the condition of their bathroom. This is the one room that can tell a person all they really need to know about you. Tub rings, toilet bowl rings, overflowing trash cans, and hair on the floor are all problem areas. The bathroom is such a personal room because it is usually where all your personal items are kept, so I keep one of my bathrooms for use as a guest bathroom only, and it should always be clean. The trash should always be emptied. Most men have horror stories about visiting a woman's home and having to use the bathroom.

I remember recently going into a girlfriend's home and there was a used panty liner in her trash basket. Now how hard is it to wrap it up so your guests don't have to look at things like that? You never know when a guest may stop in and it is so much easier when you don't have to run around making sure everything is together.

✓ **Anticipate his needs!**

Men love it when he feels that you are paying attention. I once dated a guy from Jamaica. Whenever we went out he would always order Red Stripe beer, but not many places carried it. I will never forget the first time we were hanging out at my home. He opened up the refrigerator and broke into a huge smile when he discovered I had bought his favorite Red Stripe beer. So remember that little things do count. When getting to know a man, make your home a relaxing environment. Show him that you are paying attention to the things that he enjoys, so keep the fridge stocked with his favorite food and drinks.

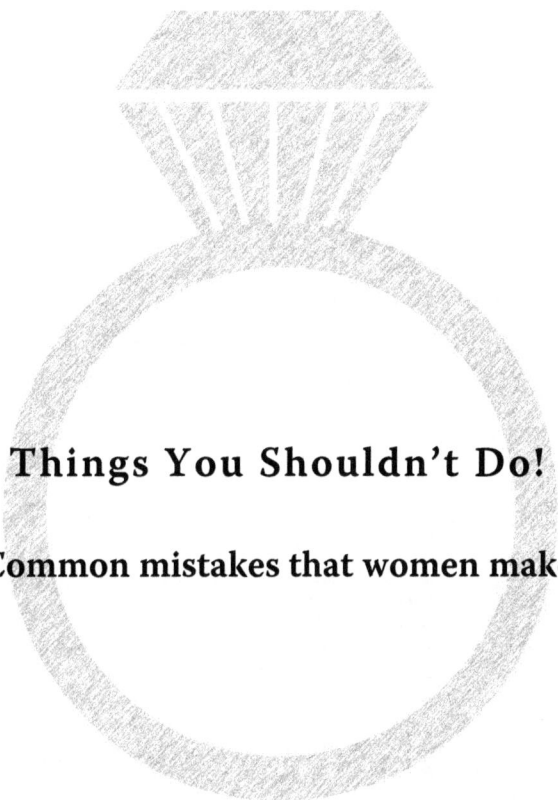

Things You Shouldn't Do!

(Common mistakes that women make)

✓ **Living together before marriage.**

Don't play house with a man. If a woman is looking for marriage, I strongly disagree with cohabiting before marriage. Too often, women put themselves in a position where they settle for living together when what they really want is the ring. If you firmly believe in marriage, don't allow your man to convince you to settle for anything less.

One woman lived with her boyfriend for twelve years. They never married. Yeah, she wanted marriage, but her man would always say the time wasn't right. He would make excuses as to why they should wait. One morning as she was putting his breakfast on the table, he told her he was leaving. He wasn't happy with her anymore and he needed some time alone. She later found out that he moved out of their home and moved in with another woman. She was devastated. She didn't know how to go on with her life because *he* was her life. She had spent twelve years making his life better. She'd made major lifestyle changes in order to be with him. She had moved away from her family and given up a well-paying job that she loved in order to relocate to be with him. Over the years, she had even used her savings and taken out loans to help him establish his business, because in the long run, it would benefit her as well. When the relationship ended, because she didn't live in a community property state, she was left with nothing. After investing twelve years into her relationship, she was starting over.

I'm not saying that shacking up is not right in every circumstance, but recognize *before* you get into the situation that the wedding ring you're looking for may never come if you choose to settle for just living together. Men ask themselves, "Why get married when you are already living like a married couple?" He's already getting all the benefits without the ring and the vows, so why would he want to change anything? Some men enjoy being in a relationship that they can walk away from with no strings attached. If something better comes along he will be free to pursue it. But there is a flip side to this situation; many couples decide to cohabitate in order to eliminate extra living expenses in preparation for their wedding. This is perfectly acceptable as long as some ground rules have already been set and you're actually moving towards a wedding date. Make sure that ring is already on your finger before you decide to live together. Keep in mind, some men use giving you a ring as a stall tactic, just to keep you quiet when he knows he has no intention of getting married. Once again, you know what you can and cannot tolerate. If you are ready and he is not, you may have to move along in order to stop him from stringing you along.

A few days ago, I spoke with a twenty-one year old woman who is currently living with her boyfriend of eighteen months. She said that she is ready for marriage, but he is not.

Recently he got tired of her bugging him about getting married, so he went out and bought her a promise ring.

You know what a promise ring says to me? It says: I promise to continue sleeping with you without the commitment of marriage, and I'm giving you this token of my affection to SHUT YOU UP!

Now, after being in a relationship with this man for eighteen months, she has earned the right to know what his hang up is and why he is not ready for marriage — especially since they are already living together.

✓ Even though you want to know don't ask!

Okay, so you've been together for a while and although it may be killing you on the inside to know if and when he will propose, *do not* verbalize those feelings. Men hate to feel pressured or pushed to do anything, even though in his mind, he may already be thinking about how and when to propose. Be patient. Don't hint or talk about it. Let him figure it out on his own. Men like to be the initiators, they want to control how and when it happens. But remember what I said earlier, when it is established that you are in an exclusive, committed relationship be up-front and let him know what your long-term goals are, that you do eventually want to get married. If he indicates that he doesn't feel the same way, or he doesn't have any interest in getting married, take him at his word and find someone who has the same wants and values as you.

Even though a man may not initially want to get married doesn't mean that he won't eventually come around to the idea. Remember, you have the power of persuasion, but you must learn how to use it. It is up to you to show him what benefit you can be as his wife. Please do not confuse what I've said here, with what I said above. The difference in these two situations is if you are or have been living together for an extended amount of time versus just casually seeing each other with no commitment. When you maintain a home together, you have a commitment and you should know where you stand.

✓ **The parent trap!**

Some women still feel that the best way to get a man to marry her is to try and trap him by getting pregnant, especially if she is involved with a successful man. Ladies, this does not work. This won't make you a wife, only a baby mama.

✓ **Trusting too quickly.**

Some women are just naturally trusting. This can be dangerous for many reasons. People take advantage of those who display a trusting nature.

For example, a sixty-seven year old co-worker developed a relationship with a twenty-six year old man who was performing community service work in her home. He was sent there by a detention center to work off his restitution. However, they developed a friendship and she soon began allowing him access to her home. She even went so far as to allow him to live there when he was released from the detention center. Within one week he had stolen all of her jewelry, a riding lawn mower and some other expensive items.

✓ **Settling for less than you're worth.**

This one needs no explanation. Never settle for less than you're worth, and you determine your worth.

✓ **The rebound syndrome.**

When you're coming off of a breakup, you need to allow yourself time to heal mentally and emotionally before getting involved in a new relationship.

✓ **Trying to change a man.**

Ladies, there are some things that you will never have control over. One of them is the ability to change another individual. Sometimes it is easy to think if you are good enough to a man he will change. But let's face the facts, the only change that you have control over is you! You can change your behavior and your way of thinking.

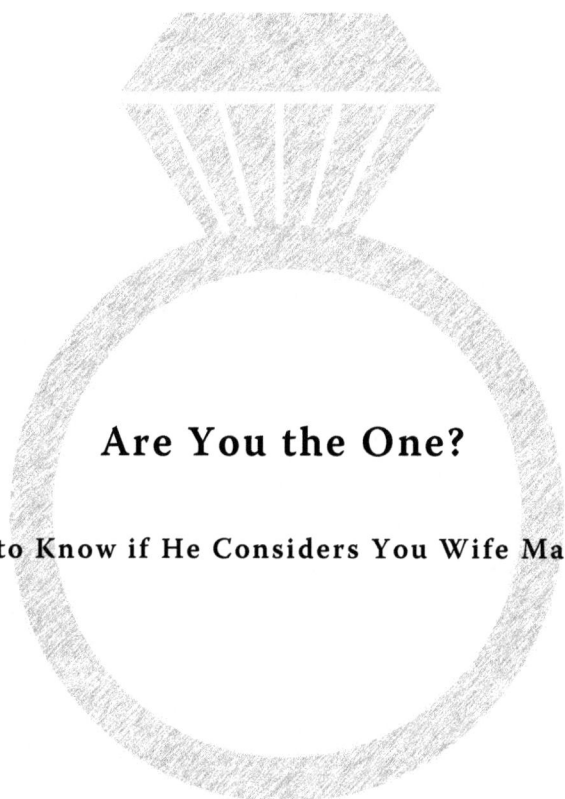

Are You the One?

(How to Know if He Considers You Wife Material)

1. When a man is in love with you there are many signs that he displays that will let you know that he considers you wife material.

2. He wants you to know his friends and family. If he has children, does he want you to meet them? Has he introduced you to his parents?

3. He wants you to interact socially with his circle of friends and willingly interacts with the people close to you.

4. You spend quality time together (outside of the bedroom).

5. He cares about your well-being. If you're sick, does he care enough to see if you're okay? (Medicine, meals, etc.)

6. He doesn't mind you leaving your stuff at his house. As a matter of fact, he encourages you to leave it. That way he knows you will be back.

7. He shows you that he is proud of your accomplish-
    ments and boasts of them to anyone he meets. He takes
    every opportunity to show you off to his friends,
    family and anyone else in his circle.

8. He's generous.

9. He speaks in terms of *we*, and *us*, instead of *I*, which
    shows he is thinking about a future with you.

10. He's not afraid and doesn't hesitate to apologize when
    he feels that he has hurt you.

11. He trusts you in his home when he's not there. You
    know your man trusts you if you spend the night at his
    place and he leaves you in bed when he goes to work
    the next morning. If a man is not into you, there is no
    way he will leave you in his home while he is not
    there. Men know that women are naturally inquisitive.
    We have a habit of going through everything, and if he
    leaves you in his home unsupervised, it means he
    trusts you.

12. He expresses his joy being in your presence. When
    you're with him he finds a reason to touch you, hold
    your hand; rest his hand on your thigh. Men are
    territorial and this is his way of showing everyone that
    you are his. Also, do his eyes follow you as you walk
    away? This behavior shows that he's into you and is
    proud to have you as his woman.

13. His friends know your name.

14. He answers his phone in your presence.

15. He checks to see that you have everything you need, including putting gas in your car.

16. He makes sacrifices for you and puts your wants and needs ahead of his own.

If your man displays any of these signs, you are definitely a keeper!

Signs That He's Not the One

art of being mentally healthy enough to be in a relationship is being smart enough to know when a situation is not healthy for you. Trust your instincts when you feel apprehensive or have doubts about a man. We talked a little bit about control in an earlier section and some of the signs you should recognize. For example, does your man display anger when he doesn't get his way? Is he easily annoyed? Does he display mood swings? Does he have outbursts of profanity at the first sign of things not going his way? These are all signs of control issues, and when a man tries to control you, it's not love.

It is up to a woman to draw the line when she sees that the relationship is not progressively moving forward. A man can and will continue to string you along if you allow it!

A common question I'm frequently asked is, "How long is too long? How long should I hang in there before giving up?"

It all depends on where you are in the relationship. Standard for me is anywhere between three to six months. For me, these are the critical months of a new relationship. It usually takes me three to six months to know if I really *like* a man. Now remember you can lust after someone and still not like them as a person. Three to six months allows you to see and get to know the real person that you are in a relationship with. Also, men usually become comfortable during this phase, so if there are any hidden girlfriend's or any other issues that you should know about, it is usually during this three to six month period that the truth comes out.

Remember that you always have a choice about who you chose to be in a relationship with. And as I said before, all relationships are not meant to result in marriage. Some relationships are meant to teach you about who you are. Not every relationship that you invest time and energy into will result in getting that ring. Because let's face it, who wants to marry someone we already know is not right for us? So there may come a point in a relationship when you realize that the man you're with is not the one. At this point you must know when to walk away. Knowing when to walk away doesn't make you a failure. It only means that you're smart.

Many times we let others dictate our actions. Remember that the people around you are on the outside looking in at your relationship. Sure, some may try to convince you of how good you have it or what a good man you have, but they are still on the outside looking in. They don't know what goes on inside your home. They only know what you tell them. It may even be your man who is trying to convince you how good you have it, but only you know what you can and cannot deal with. The day you start allowing your man to dictate your life, you give up your independence.

Another thing that I'm frequently asked is, "If my man has cheated, should I stay and try to work through it?" That is a call that you must make by looking at the circumstances and evaluating where you are in your relationship or marriage. I personally don't think that I could ever trust again after having been betrayed, but some women can. I do, however, feel that if you can salvage your relationship and not compromise yourself, then maybe you should try to do it.

Everyone is human and we do make mistakes, so just because a man may have made a decision that disappoints you, doesn't make him a loser or a bad person. He just made a bad decision. If, at any point, you decide that it is time to move on, then that's what you must do.

One of the reasons that break ups are so hard is because we hate starting over. Sometimes when we are afraid of the unknown, it is easier to hang on to something that is familiar. When you have been with a man for any length of time it can be hard to let go. But the next time you say you can't live without him, ask yourself how much *living* are you really doing with him?

When ending a relationship, be mindful of the other person's feelings. Words do hurt and sometimes if you choose the wrong words, the one ending up hurt could be you. Too often we hear of women who tried to leave only to have a situation escalate, which resulted in someone ending up hurt or dead. Do everything in your power to avoid being in this situation. I know firsthand how trying to leave a man can end up violent. I have witnessed men who never had any violent tendencies in their life suddenly turn violent. And normally it starts out over a situation that got completely out of hand.

If you find yourself in a situation that has become ugly, do not throw around hateful words. Telling a man who is really into you that you don't want him anymore is all it takes for some men to snap. If you should happen to find yourself in a situation that could potentially become violent, remain calm and speak in a calm tone of voice. Don't engage in verbal banter. Do not get into a mudslinging match with a man. It's not worth it. One thing always leads to another, which could cause the problem to escalate. And in some cases, it may be necessary to tell that individual that you're trying to get away from whatever he wants to hear to give yourself an opportunity to get away from him. So, if it takes reassuring him that you won't leave him, reassure him and as soon as possible, get out.

Some women may not be aware that they do enjoy emotionally painful relationships. The person that we are comfortable with tells us a lot about ourselves. If a woman continues to allow someone to abuse her, whether physically, verbally, or emotionally, there are problems. There is the possibility that she enjoys abusive relationships.

We normally emulate the environment in which we grew up in. If you were raised in a household where abuse was prevalent between your parents, you might think abusive behavior is normal. But it's not! Healthy relationships are built on mutual respect and mutual respect is needed in order for a relationship to survive. Respect means that your man understands and values who you are and would never challenge your boundaries.

Is 365 Days Really Enough Time?

*W*hen I speak of getting that ring in 365 days or less, I'm not necessarily talking about taking the vows of marriage in 365 days or less. However, you can have a proposal of marriage within that time frame. And yes, ladies, if you don't already have the ring by this time you should know that it is on the way!

I Followed All the Rules, but Still No Ring

adies, it happens sometimes. You might do all the right things and he still won't marry you. If this is the case, be assured that it's not because of something that you've done wrong. He's just not the man for you. As with my friend Jessica's case, don't waste precious years of your life waiting for a man to marry you. It doesn't take years for a man to know if he wants you as his wife. If you are not good enough to be his wife, then you shouldn't be good enough to continue giving him privileges like you are his wife.

When you feel that you have done all that you can do and your man is still not showing any signs of heading towards the altar, there comes a point when he needs to shit or you need to push his ass off the pot. Although you cannot control a man's actions, you can control whether or not you allow him to keep you hanging on for an indefinite amount of time without proposing to you.

If It's Not Working,
How Do I Get Over Him?

This section is important to me for many reasons. Because I have been married and divorced five times, women who know me know that I have no problem leaving a relationship that is not working. Women frequently ask me how can I walk away from a man and never look back.

Look at it this way. Your whole purpose in reading this book was to learn how to get him to put that ring on your finger in 365 days or less. Guess what? If it didn't happen your mission wasn't accomplished. And it could be because he's telling you verbally, or by action, that he doesn't want a relationship with you.

Rejection is nothing to be ashamed of. Remember, every experience brought into your life plays a critical role in your personal growth and development. Welcome those experiences, for they were meant to teach you about yourself. As I said earlier, all relationships are not meant to result in marriage. There are many men who want the same things that you do, they want marriage and commitment. So if the man you are with turns out to be a dud, let him go. Free yourself, so that when your Mr. Right does happen along, you will be ready.

How to Deal With Rejection

ejection by the one you love is the most powerful destroyer of self-esteem. But it is a part of life and at some point it happens to everyone. Don't ever feel like you are losing something because a man doesn't want to be with you.

Let me tell you a story. When I was in my early twenties, after my second marriage ended, I was involved with a wonderful man. He was funny, compassionate and so giving of himself. He was a successful business owner and we did everything together. We enjoyed weekend getaways and the sex was absolutely amazing. There was no doubt that I cared deeply for him.

At the time, I was working as a manager of a local dollar store and his business wasn't far from my job. I was so into this man that we were spending every night together, then getting up and going to work at the same time. At lunchtime, it was normal for us to have lunch together if he wasn't busy with a client. It was common for me to arrange my lunch schedule around him. One particular day, after we had spent a wonderful night together and both gone in to work, I paged him to see what his plans were for lunch as I did every day.

When he called me back, he was so cold and unfeeling, and this wasn't normal behavior for him, so I was concerned.

He rudely asked me why I called his pager when I knew he was at work. I replied that I didn't want to interrupt him if he was in the middle of a job. I was concerned because he sounded so angry. I couldn't understand how someone who had just held me so tenderly through the night could suddenly become this cold and unfeeling person that I was speaking to. So I asked, "Honey, are you okay?"

And he said to me, "My name is *not* honey, it's Quincy!"

Wow! I was blown away. I felt like someone had doused my body with ice water. His whole demeanor had changed. Suddenly he said to me, "I don't want this anymore!" and he hung up.

My whole body went cold and I immediately called him back, but he wouldn't accept my calls. I left work and went the few blocks to his office. He was working on a job and he wouldn't even acknowledge me, let alone talk to me. After trying to get him to tell what was going on, with no results, I finally gave up and left with a hole in my heart. The only thing I could process in my head was, "How could he not want me?" No matter how hard I tried, I couldn't fathom this. In my mind, I went back over the conversations that we'd had, trying to figure out if I had said or done something to provoke him. Because he wouldn't talk to me, and tell me what the problem was, I had to try to figure it out on my own. No matter how I tried, I couldn't fit the pieces together. The most logical reason that I could come up with was that he had found someone else, and that hurt.

Over the course of the next few days it seemed that the more he ignored me, the more determined I was to make him love me. I became obsessed. I would drive past his home, his office…I was crazy. It was aggravating the heck out of me that I didn't know what was going on in his mind. And it hurt because he acted like we had never happened.

Suddenly, one day after about three weeks of this madness. I learned a powerful lesson. I realized that although I didn't have closure to the relationship, I was a strong woman and I loved myself. Even if for some unknown reason he no longer loved me. The reason for his behavior didn't matter anymore. I finally recognized my worth and what I brought into that relationship. I realized I didn't deserve to be treated the way he was treating me. For three weeks I had survived without him and I was okay. I didn't die, I had survived.

Once I recognized my worth, I developed a different attitude towards him. I realized that he didn't deserve me. When I learned this powerful lesson I stopped calling him. I stopped driving past his house and business. I stopped my obsessive behavior, because, ladies, you know we can develop obsessive behavior. And when I stopped, the strangest thing happened. The roles reversed. He started ringing my phone off the hook, driving past my house and coming into my job with the pretense of conducting business. Now he wanted to talk. He wanted to explain, but at this point, it didn't even matter anymore. I had moved on. He could not understand how he had lost his hold over me.

Ladies, sometimes we too freely give up the control of our life to a man. We work our daily activities around *his* schedule. We make ourselves available to *him* when *he's* ready and when it's convenient for him. In order to get back to being me, I had to take back control of my life. I realized that it didn't matter why he didn't want me, so when he finally decided that he needed to explain, I didn't want to hear it and I refused to listen. In my mind, I had moved on and I didn't want to hear his excuses for treating me so badly.

A few years ago, I happened to be in town and stopped by his business. When I walked in, it was like he was looking at a ghost. He grabbed me and lifted me up in the air in a bear hug. He held me without saying a word for a full ten minutes before he let me go. It was an emotional and joyful reunion. After sixteen years, we finally had the conversation we should have had a decade earlier.

During the time that he and I were seeing each other, although I was separated from my then husband, I wasn't divorced. He said, "I was sleeping with you every night and technically you were still married to another man. It was killing me inside!" He felt I had no intention of divorcing my husband and he was tired of waiting, so he wanted to hurt me like I had hurt him.

It took sixteen years for the true problem to emerge. Back then, instead of being honest with me about what his problem actually was, he kept it inside. When all he ever had to do was be honest and express his feelings to me. What he didn't understand was that during that time, I had already filed for a divorce, and anyone who has ever experienced divorce knows how long the process can be, but he just didn't get it. To think, we could have saved each other a lot of heartache just by communicating.

Things that Men Dislike in a Woman!

$\mathcal{A}$s an author I'm known for doing a lot of social networking. I have many websites and blog sites that cater mostly to women's issues. After a while, men started sending me letters and emails asking, "Why do you cater only to women's issues? Why don't you have a site that caters to men?" So I decided to create a forum where men could express themselves. One of the things I asked was what turned men off about a woman. I sent out questionnaires to men ranging in ages from twenty-four to sixty and this is what they had to say.

The following list is a result of that topic:

- ✓ **Withholding sex as a form of punishment.**

This was addressed in a previous section, so I don't think this one requires any further explanation.

- ✓ **Words do hurt!**

So be careful of what you say even if you're angry. Words can't be taken back, even if you are forgiven for saying hurtful things.

✓ **Do not question or threaten his manhood!**

✓ **Materialistic behavior or Gold diggers ~ women who use men for personal gain.**

Okay, so we know that there are a lot of materialistic women out there. These women prey on men not for who they are, but for what they can provide to them. However, men need to realize that not every woman is out for something.

✓ **Nagging.**

Men sometimes say that their women have a habit of making demands, so he'll say that she's nagging. I personally have a problem with this term. I feel that nagging is a term that men created to describe an action by a woman who incessantly asks something of him that he doesn't want to do or that he can't do. But I find it funny that when men ask women to do something, they're not nagging, they just expect an immediate response.

Perfect example, this is an actual email from one of my female readers.

Ms. Wallace,

My mom invited my boyfriend and me to a family function and asked if we would be able to attend. Of course I told her I needed to check with him first to see if it was acceptable before I committed to it. When I told my boyfriend about the invitation, he said he would let me know in a few days, not caring that my mom is still waiting for a response. Every day I ask him if he's made up his mind about my mom's invitation and he just ignores me. A few days ago his best friend invited us to his mom's 70th birthday party, which just happens to fall on the same day as my mom's family function. He accepted the invitation for the both of us without checking to see if I wanted to attend. And he still hasn't acknowledged the fact that my mom is still waiting for a response! How should I handle this situation?

Dear Reader:

Your boyfriend shows an obvious disregard for your feelings. I'm not sure how to address this because I'm not sure if this is your boyfriend's character all the time, or if this was just a random incident. My gut instinct tells me that it is not a random incident. Men who display this type of behavior usually don't deviate from their way of life to suit anyone, not even his woman. However, there are several ways that you can handle this situation. You can either tell him that you will attend your mom's function without him and he can attend his friend's mother's birthday party without you, or you can do what I would do in this situation. Tell him nothing! Let him think you're going to his friend's mother's party with him. Get all "sexied" up in that favorite sexy outfit that he loves to see you in, and as you're going out the door to your mom's function, give him a big kiss and tell him to have a great time at the party! Let him think about that while he's partying with the seventy year olds! Good luck, lady!

I get letters like this all the time, but because I was addressing the subject of *nagging* I couldn't help but share this one with you. Okay, back to the list!

✓ **Attitudes.**

Men don't find women who come across as snotty or uppity, attractive. Most men also included women who are vain, loud and obnoxious, in this category.

✓ **Argumentative.**

Women who can (and will) argue about anything.

✓ **Clingy and dependent.**

Men enjoy the company of women who have a life of their own. Having other interests is what keeps a man interested in a woman. Men love women who are intelligent, independent, and able to hold their own.

✓ **Low self-esteem.**

Men do not want a woman who lacks confidence. If a woman has self-esteem issues he fears he will spend too much unnecessary time reassuring her of her worth.

✓ **Dishonesty.**

Lying is not sexy or necessary.

✓ **No interest in sex.**

If you missed it in the section *Let's Talk About SEX* It might be a good idea to go back and check it out.

✓ **Body odor.**

If he can't get up close and personal with it, he doesn't want it!

✓ **Selfishness.**

Women who expect her man to do everything for her, yet she refuses to contribute anything.

✓ **Immaturity.**

Women who resort to petty tactics to get what they want.

✓ **Women who smoke.**

There is nothing less attractive than a woman with a cigarette dangling from her lips! Except maybe a woman who is sloppy drunk!

To Sum It All Up!

inally, we have come to the end of our journey! Look at where you are in your life right now. Although last week may have been horrible, this week doesn't have to be. Life gives us many opportunities to start again and improve on the things that we may not be happy or satisfied with. Each new day is another opportunity to change what you didn't like about your life yesterday. No matter where you are right here today, it is never too late to make a change for the better.

I know that after reading this book, some women (especially you independent women), are probably sitting around right now saying, "How is this going to help me get that ring on my finger in 365 days or less? Why should I have to cater to an overgrown man child in order to get him to put a ring on my finger?"

Ladies, for a man, the greatest feeling in the world is being appreciated by the woman he loves. When you give him that he will give you the world. Men are tired of hearing that same old "I am woman, hear me roar" song. If you consider yourself to be Ms. Independent and can do *everything* for yourself, then clearly you don't need a man, so this book wouldn't apply to you.

The greatest thing about this world we live in is that nobody can force you to do anything. However, if you keep doing things the same way, you're going to continue having the same results. Getting a man to put that ring on your finger in 365 days or less comes with changing the way you think, thereby, changing your attitude.

In this book, you have all the knowledge you need to achieve your mission. When you use the information outlined in this book to *develop* this attitude, you will have mastered *How to Get Him to Put That Ring on Your Finger In 365 Days or Less!*

After reading all the rules outlined in this book, you should now be prepared to get your man. Ultimately, there are three key things that will increase your value to your man.

- *You* have the ability to make your man feel like *Superman*; so never fail to be his own personal cheerleader!

- Appeal to his sexual side. If he is a good man, never say the word *no*!

- Being his partner means having yourself together physically, mentally, and financially!

I genuinely care about the success of each and every one of you! So be sure to write me and let me know how you're doing. And just in case you're getting married as a result of this book, please send me a wedding invitation!

About the Author

Glenda A. Wallace is the Founder & CEO of several businesses under Pink Kiss Enterprise. She founded Pink Kiss Publishing Company in 2008. In addition to being a publisher, she is an author, entrepreneur, educator and creative consultant.

Ms. Wallace is dedicated to uplifting, inspiring and empowering women to discover their true potential, so that they may achieve the highest level of success. She lives, works and plays on the beautiful Mississippi Gulf Coast.

Please visit her website @ www.pinkkisspublishing.com

Thanks for your support! And don't forget, I'd love to hear from you! So please leave a review!

Also by Glenda A. Wallace

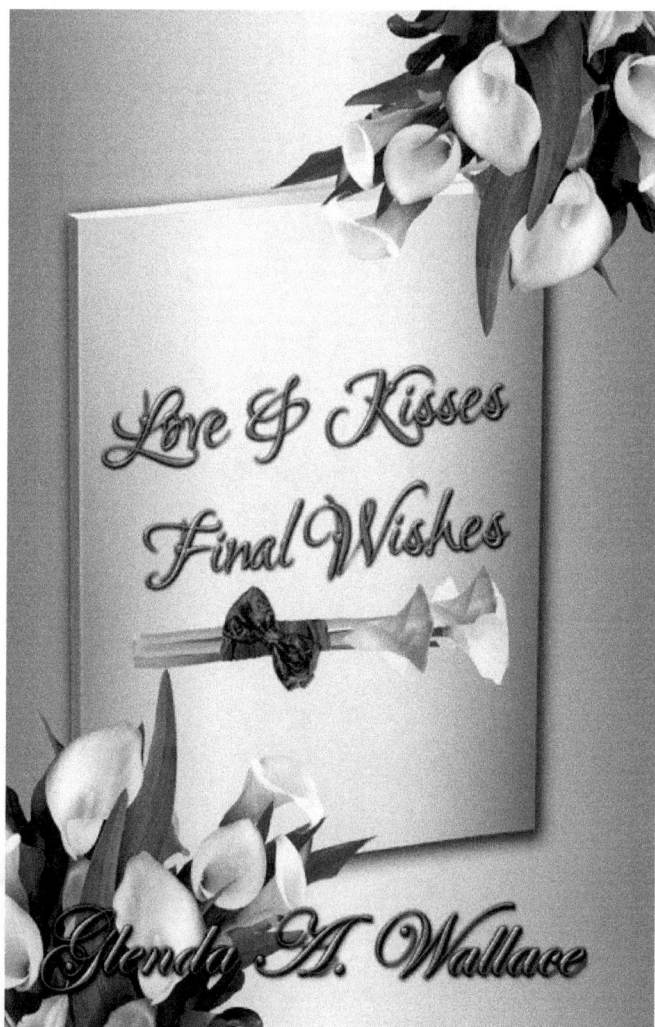

Love & Kisses Final Wishes

Glenda A. Wallace

Married, But Single!

Glenn a S

Coming Soon

What Every Teenage Girl
Should Know...
About
Boys, Sex, Love and Life in General!

Glenda A. Wallace

Do you have a story just waiting to be brought to life that you'd like to share with the world? Of course you do! We all have something valuable to share with others that someone can learn from. If you're interested in publishing opportunities we'd love to hear from you. To learn more, please visit our publishing services page at:

www.pinkkisspublishing.com/Your-Book-Your-Way-.html

Or contact Glenda Wallace at:
glendawallace@pinkkisspublishing.com

You can also reach us by phone at 228-366-6829 or by fax at 228-205-3610.

Thanks again for your support!

www.ingramcontent.com/pod-product-compliance
Lightning Source LLC
LaVergne TN
LVHW051459080426
835509LV00017B/1832